Advanced Praise for

# Notes from a
# Beijing Coffeeshop

"The personal stories from survivors of the Cultural Revolution will stop you in your tracks but so will the sheer determination of today's generation - Lanna, fighting for her female voice to be heard, or Sing, surely China's only hi-tech raspberry grower.

*Notes from a Beijing Coffeeshop* is like Dim Sum - bite-sized pieces of China that whet your appetite and leave you wanting more."

Hilary East, Avenue53 Consulting Ltd

"There are many books that try to help Westerners to understand China, but few which tell the story of the dreams and aspirations, and the realities of life, from a Chinese perspective.

A fascinating and well researched insight into life in China today."

Nigel Ruddock, Chairman, Grant Thornton Singapore

"I have been involved with *Notes from a Beijing Coffeeshop* since the beginning. Jonathan was keen to do another book on China as a follow up the widely acclaimed Thoughts of Chairmen Now and over numerous cups of coffee when he was in London, he would talk to me about what he wanted this book to be about.

In his own inimitable way, Jonathan has explored China in ways few people have. He has met fascinating people from all walks of life and each of them has a captivating story. Jonathan wanted to tell these stories to a wider western audience so that we would gain an insight into a culture that can seem impenetrable but which we need to understand better."

*Notes from a Beijing Coffeeshop* gets under the skin of China by using powerful human truths to bring to life the facts and figures we read about daily. I read the entire book in one night and found it completely absorbing. I subsequently re-read the stories I found most interesting and you will too.

Anyone interested in China must read it and even those who know the country well will learn something new."

**Paul Gordon,** Managing Director Autotorq and
International Business Consultant

"This book is absorbing. The human stories give an insight into China and Chinese society that is unique and it is essential reading for anyone interested in this amazing country."

Jonathan Lord, MP

"This absorbing book is an essential read, offering insight into a world that fascinates and baffles. Over cups of coffee, Geldart gently probes representatives of modern China, encouraging them to open up and share. It is the combination of big dreams and ordinary detail that startles and charms – if you ever do business in Beijing, don't schedule an important meeting on the 4th."

**Kate Manasian,** Manasian and Co

"I have been in business for many years and retirement beckons. China has grown massively during that time and like many of my contemporaries I have observed it from the corner of my eye and concluded that it is 'too difficult" or "too complex' to understand. Leave that to others.

This book changes all that. It is gentle, thoughtful and very readable. Because it is written from the heart I can believe it and engage with it. It makes me want to learn more about China and its people. And perhaps it might give me the confidence to go there soon.

If you want to really start to understand China, read this book! And then prepare to drink a lot of coffee and have the experience of a lifetime."

**Richard Morrice,** Director - Independent Drinks

"*Notes from a Beijing Coffeeshop* offers a fascinating account of China, told through seemingly casual interviews with Chinese citizens. Jonathan gets to the heart of a wide range of topics with his interview partners from China's middle class. Every interview offers particular insights into China today while in particular the longer interviews impress through their account of China's economic and social development. Notes provides insights into how Chinese people think and what makes their businesses so successful."

Hinrich Voss, Lecturer in International Business at Leeds University Business School & Director Business Confucius Institute at the University of Leeds

"This book provides a fascinating insight into a wide cross section of people from retired government officials to emerging entrepreneurs. The stories from the front line of business will provide entrepreneurs from the UK and elsewhere with an informative backdrop should they be interested in trying to set up or do business in China."

Hamish Stevenson, founder & CEO of Fast Track, and associate fellow, Green Templeton College, Oxford University

'China, to most of us, remains a puzzle. However, by recording his many relaxed, open and remarkably frank conversations with a fascinating cross-section of 'Beijingers' - all of whom have lived through dramatic changes in their society - Jonathan Geldart has both illustrated how different to the West life is in China, but also how much the people's fears, hopes and aspirations are the same. These conversations, over endless cups of coffee, in a subtle, charming , very effective way, open a window onto their lives. If you want to understand much more about life in modern, urban China - read this book.'

David McDonnell, Pro-Chancellor , University of Liverpool

# Notes
## from a
# Beijing
# Coffeeshop

Insights into modern China —
A collection of personnal stories

Published by
LID Publishing Ltd
One Mercer Street, Covent Garden,
London, Wc2H 9JQ

31 West 34th Street, Suite 7004,
New York, NY 10001, US

info@lidpublishing.com
www.lidpublishing.com

A member of:

BPR
Business Publishers Roundtable

www.businesspublishersroundtable.com

Printed in Great Britain by TJ International
ISBN: 978-1-910649-14-5

Cover and page design: Laura Hawkins

# Notes

## from a

# Beijing

# Coffeeshop

Insights into modern China —
A collection of personnal stories

## Jonathan Geldart

LONDON      MONTERREY
MADRID      SHANGHAI
MEXICO CITY  BOGOTA
NEW YORK    BUENOS AIRES
BARCELONA   SAN FRANCISCO

To Clare.

We make a great team... thank you

# Contents

# Foreword

I met Jonathan through a mutual business associate who felt our shared fascination with China could lead to an interesting discussion over lunch. In fact, it led to a book, *The Thoughts of Chairmen Now*, a unique look at business in China, which we co-authored and first published in late 2013 and reprinted in 2015.

Jonathan and I share a passion for China. Its fast-growing and vibrant economy has created some of the greatest and most valuable brands on the planet, of which many people in the rest of the world have never heard. In addition, its long history and fascinating culture have absorbed and captivated us both. However, it is the daily interaction with ordinary people that is the most compelling aspect of living and working there. This book of 'Notes' is the product of many hours of meetings and I hate to think how much coffee! It tells some of the stories of those ordinary people. You will find a full range of experiences and emotions, lessons and insights enshrined not only in the words of the people but also in the personal notes and commentary from Jonathan.

I have been particularly impressed by how Jonathan has obtained access to these people and how they have opened up to him and shared their stories. The Chinese are often thought to be "closed" and difficult to read. These Notes are anything but.

Through a series of, sometimes impromptu, interviews Jonathan has let the voice of ordinary Chinese people be heard. I recognize many of the stories as I too have heard them told across China during my many years in the country, but I never recorded them. I am glad that Jonathan has. They deserve to be told and the insights they uncover to be explored.

David Roth
CEO, The Store Worldwide WPP Group

# Frontispiece

Having spent more than five years in Beijing, at first as a 'fly in' and 'fly out' visitor, and more recently, feeling much more like a resident, I have developed a survival strategy as a 'laowai', 'waiguo ren" or foreigner in this fast moving, heavily polluted capital:

Coffee

I started with Starbucks and moved through McDonalds (once was enough) to Costa and even Subway (once). Now I have settled in one place to indulge my two vices: working on the internet when the office system throws me out (frequently); and coffee.

I was never really a big coffee drinker and, of course, tea is the thing in China, but I just can't help myself. Also the place in which I have now landed, and my favourite, where most of my meetings and conversations seem to take place, is an eclectic mix of Chinese tea house and Western coffee shop. It provides as much breakfast as you can eat for ¥50 (£5.50) (most of it actually edible) and very passable coffee, pretty much on tap for ¥20 (£2.20) a mug. I have settled here in my, now well-established, seat next to the window. It is under the air con (essential in a Beijing summer) and just over the main heater pipe (just as essential in the bitter Beijing winter). Here, over the past year, I have met a wide variety of people, of all ages, not only from around China but around the world. The block above houses a series of apartments, variously let to lower-tier diplomatic staff from places as varied as Korea and Japan as well as the Ukraine, Kazakhstan and a couple of Central African countries whose names and locations their staff still have not admitted to.

It is here my notes have been made, initially for personal use and then as the basis of my last book, *The Thoughts of Chairmen Now,* 2013. However, many of the stories of ordinary Chinese people, business leaders, and opinion formers, who I have enticed in to speak to me, have not been told before. It remains a total mystery to me why these people agreed to tell me their stories, and even more so that they were happy for me to write them down. Some have asked to remain anonymous, but most were happy to be quoted and even photographed.

These are not the deranged ramblings of a disordered mind, though some of the stories are quite amazing. They are all true and real. The people are real, the stories are real and the places are real. The result is a perspective on China I believe is a little different. The notes are a compilation of a series of my personal insights into Chinese life, Chinese business and Chinese culture through the eyes and mouths of the Chinese people who live and work here. It is also their perspectives on the Western world. There is nothing particularly new in the stories of these people, but it is the first time their stories have been told. The comments and reflections which accompany their words are my own, drawn from a good deal of additional listening and personal experiences in China, and specifically, Beijing. I have listened hard and reflected at length both on what was said to me, and the window into ordinary Chinese life that the words opened. If I have misinterpreted any comments or missed important things, then I apologize unreservedly.

These Notes are not only reflections on the words of those to whom I spoke, but also my personal commentary on modern China as it appears to me every day I am here.

# Introduction

I have found that, despite all the reading and preparation many people do before arriving in China, be it for a holiday or for business, nothing really prepares them for the layers of subtlety and complexity that is everyday life here. I have learned more by living, working, eating, drinking, oh and singing, here with Chinese colleagues and friends, than any book or tourist trail guide could ever have taught me. The more I listen, the more I learn and the more I learn, the more I appreciate that I know so little about this sometimes strange and contradictory country.

This book is an effort to allow what I believe to be the real China, behind the rhetoric of the media and the stereotypes of prejudice, to emerge through the words of ordinary citizens. True, they are almost all living and working in Beijing, but they are predominantly not 'Beijingers' 'Beijing ren' or 'Beijing people' in Chinese. Beijing is the political heart of China. It is also a magnet for everyone across the country who see its streets as the place to make money and seek their fortune. While Shanghai is often perceived as the international centre, and there are many cities and places across China which are very different, the capital has a quality all its own. It is a melting pot of Chinese from all provinces and ethnicities. It is Chinese. Foreigners are very much in the smallest of minorities, and as such, unlike so many of the capitals of the world, Beijing is a more accurate cultural barometer of the country than you may find in the likes of Washington DC, London, Paris or Berlin.

There are insights here on all aspects of Chinese life should you choose to pause and reflect on them. There are stories of marriage, of gender inequality, of business strategy and gay rights. It is a deliberate mixture of every aspect of China.

The reader should also be aware of a few other aspects of Beijing life, which may help in their understanding and appreciation of some of the stories. These are my personal observations and will probably not be found in any guidebook. Throughout these notes there are repeated references to a number of key aspects of Chinese and Beijing life. To help the reader understand these better I have provided some additional explanations here:

The 'Hukou' 户口) is referred to often. This is the certificate of residence that every Chinese person possesses. It divides those from the cities from those in the rural areas. It denotes where he or she lives; their 'home town'. The Hukou is probably the single most important document possessed by any Chinese person.

It used to be that having no Hukou meant you received no food coupons and in the Cultural Revolution, that meant you starved. Today those with a rural Hukou are treated differently from those with one from a city, specifically the larger ones, such as Beijing or Shanghai, who are afforded additional privileges in terms of job opportunities, pensions, medical support and education. The information stored on your identity card is based on your Hukou.

People complain about the pollution in Beijing. It is not good in many cities but Beijing is the capital and bears the brunt of the criticism and noise. I can attest that it is terrible and everyone complains about it. Most days, it exceeds all World Health Organisation guidelines for air worth breathing. About 95% of the population don't bother to wear protective face masks and those that are for sale seem to be more decorative than effective. The masks that are recommended to keep out the worst of the airborne micro-soot which can clog your lungs are expensive and usually out of stock (if they ever were in stock in the first place). Everyone complains, but we all just suffer and those who can afford to do so buy air filters for their house. Those who can't, just accept it. You can tell the good days as you can see the mountains that ring Beijing to the west and north. You can tell the bad days as you can't see the buildings over the road!

The subway is amazing: fast, efficient, on time and air-conditioned, but the crush of humanity is overwhelming during rush hours, which last from around 07.30 to 09.00 and 18.00 to 19.30. The rest of the time it is just bad, then it shuts. The authorities are building more and more lines, there are 18 currently. At the end of 2014, there were almost 300 stations and more are scheduled. More than 10 million people use the subway each day, and it feels like it. It is incredibly cheap with a base cost of ¥3 (£0.33) and only ¥10 (£1.10) for the longest of journeys. Once you learn to navigate the labyrinth of intersecting lines and connecting access tunnels it gets you to most places, most of the time. Link that to the buses, which are even cheaper and go to more inaccessible locations, and you are transported round the city with a surprising degree of ease. The longer distance buses will take you out to the suburbs an hour away for ¥20 (£2.20) and even further if you can bear the commute. Many do.

Taxis are the other heavily subsidised transportation in Beijing. For less than ¥30 (£3.40) you can cross the city and for ¥100 (£11) make it out to the airport from the centre, including the road toll of ¥10 (£1.10). They are everywhere but have no obligation to stop and pick you up if they don't want to. Foreigners are studiously avoided by many as no driver I have had pick me up has ever spoken English and they don't want the hassle. You soon learn to stand waving a piece of paper in your hand as they assume it is an address. Drivers are usually visibly relieved and thankful if you get in speaking even basic Chinese.

Traffic in Beijing is a nightmare. The main routes are clogged and fume-ridden from early morning to late at night. Of course many cities around the globe are the same, but you would have thought that, with arterial expressways, of which there are many, having three lanes each way and a bus lane as well, this would be enough to whisk you round the city with consummate ease. You'd be wrong. The traffic crawls and snarls its way through the wide streets and narrow ones at the same frustrating snail's pace. Three lanes often are made into four by impatient drivers. Indicators are seemingly decorative and driving quality appalling, which makes the whole experience more an application of sixth sense and blind faith over rules and standards. Accidents are rare, but insurance rarer still. If there is an accident, everything stops where it is, in the fast lane sometimes, while it is all sorted out, with or without police involvement.

For businesses, most people will only schedule two meetings a day in Beijing, one in the morning and one in the late afternoon. The traffic is the main reason for the scheduling. Arriving on time is difficult and lateness often accepted, if accompanied with a rolling of the eyes and a "the traffic was terrible" comment. If a meeting is scheduled for 11.00 or later, you will probably go to lunch together; if later in the afternoon, then dinner is quite likely. If dinner is for business purposes, then drink yoghurt! It lines the stomach and offers some small protection against the Baijiu (白酒) or strongly distilled spirit you will almost certainly be served.

Lunch in China is at noon and the entire country stops to eat. Watching millions of people being served at the same time is a sight worth seeing. There are food stalls and restaurants of every size, type and taste everywhere. Be aware that eating food is about relationship building, not usually discussing business. In the evening, dinner will start at 18.00 or perhaps 19.00 and you'll be done by 21.30. If red wine and Baijiu-toasting has been involved, then you really will be 'done' by 21.30. There can often be an invitation to karaoke after food and you should be prepared to be singing "Hey Jude" at the top of your voice with a bunch of spirited, often spirit-fuelled, colleagues until the early hours. I find I have learned to develop recurring heartburn and to retire early.

Relationships (guanxi 关系) are critical in China. They drive every aspect of business and social interaction. They are built over considerable time and with effort. Don't expect to do anything, particularly business, if you have not expended time on building the personal relationships first. It may seem like you are wasting time. You are not. Long-lasting relationships will open doors you never knew existed. Most business deals I have seen fail have done so on the back of Westerners trying to short-cut the relationship-building. Also, relationships are passed from one person to another. So if you are introduced by one person to another, they are showing you a lot of 'face' (see below) and, as such, you should treat the new 'friend' with the same respect as your mutual contact. Relationships build up a web of connections which will serve you well in getting on in China, from helping you find a good place to eat, to doing a deal. Do not underestimate their power or importance.

The notion of 'face' (面子 mian zi) in China is often referred to and a reference here is important. The idea of 'face' is disarmingly simple. It is about showing the right level of respect to others. No one likes to be embarrassed, especially in front of friends or colleagues and this is no less the case in China than anywhere else in the world. However, it is a bit easier to make a mistake in China due to the complexity of the culture and layers of meaning attached to so many things. In addition, people can take offence at things that Westerners shrug off as either unimportant or irrelevant. It is possible to step on a cultural or social 'landmine' without even knowing it has gone off, until you are refused another meeting or find people politely but permanently 'unavailable'. The simple rule is be polite to everyone. It costs nothing and pays dividends. Also pay attention as much to what is not said as to what is. Reading between the lines is an art form in China and it is easy to make mistakes here too, on both sides. Be as precise and explicit about what you mean as possible, to avoid ambiguity. There is an assumption by most Chinese people, who might not have experienced a Western culture before, that you will be meaning something additional to your words when you speak. If you feel there may be something being left unsaid, it probably is. Asking outright for clarification will be taken as a loss of 'face' so be sure to have someone around to 'interpret' for you as well as 'translate'.

The Chinese can be incredibly direct, which can be seen as 'rude', in the eyes of many Westerners. I have often had someone look me in the eye, and without a shred of irony, ask why my hair is grey and why I don't dye it black, like every other senior leader in China. I just smile and apologize for being English! People will comment on your hair, clothes, taste in food, use of cosmetics, or accent, without a blink of the eye. Sometimes it is to tell you that you look good, but not always. My advice here is to roll with the punches. It is not meant badly and to respond negatively will be to tread on the broken glass of 'face'.

Finally, from a business – and indeed a social – perspective gifts are important in China. At the root of this is the notion of 'face' and respect but it is also simply that we all appreciate people being thoughtful. Gifting has had a bad name in China in recent years as extravagant gifts were connected to the corruption and 'graft' the current leadership is fighting to destroy. However, the giving and receiving of small, inexpensive, but thoughtful gifts is really appreciated and reciprocated. Not to do so could well be taken badly, unless you know each other well and agree that gifts are unnecessary for each visit. But don't forget gifts at the major festivals or it will go down very poorly! My habit now is to take sweets from my home town in the north of England. Most Chinese people have a very sweet tooth and the personal connection is understood and always elicits smiles. You may well end up with a lot of tea in return, but it makes great 'regifting' presents for those at home and everyone understands that there is only so much tea you can drink.

The Chinese have been trying, for more than 2,000 years, since the Qin Dynasty, to organize their enormous country into some form of hierarchy. The government today divides the People's Republic of China into five administrative divisions, roughly based on geography and population: province, prefecture, county, township and village. Separately, and with some overlap, an unofficial system organizes cities into Tiers. This is based, in part, on size, but mostly on economic development. Despite its shortcomings, the Tier system is a useful classification device. The municipalities of Beijing, Shanghai, Guangzhou and Shenzhen are widely referenced as being 'Tier 1' cities. There are 32 'Tier 2' cities and provincial capitals (roughly), 238 prefecture cities at 'Tier 3' and 383 county cities at 'Tier 4'. A remaining group of around 1,643 towns are said to be 'Tier 5'. I am indebted to research by Millward Bown, a WPP research company, for this definition.

Of course, I could go on. And on. But suffice to say that you can browse many books and the internet to learn more about Chinese history and culture. I advise that you do. Even a broad understanding of the long and complex history of China will be very much appreciated. At the end of the day, however, no one expects you to be Chinese.

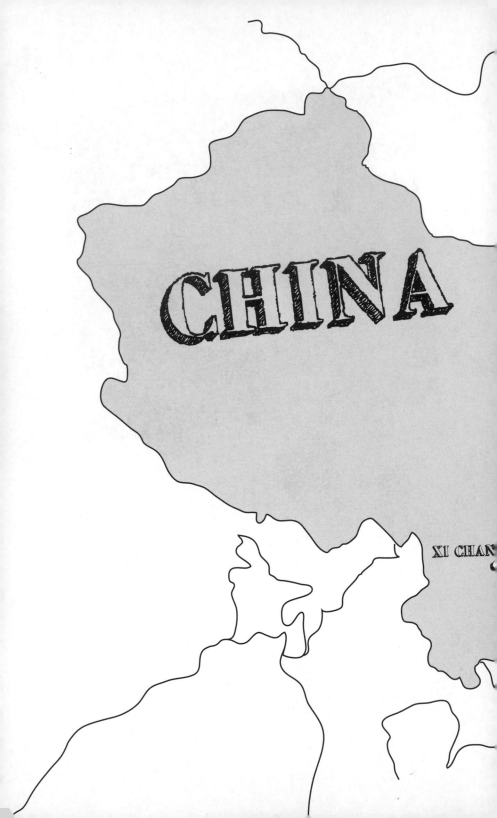

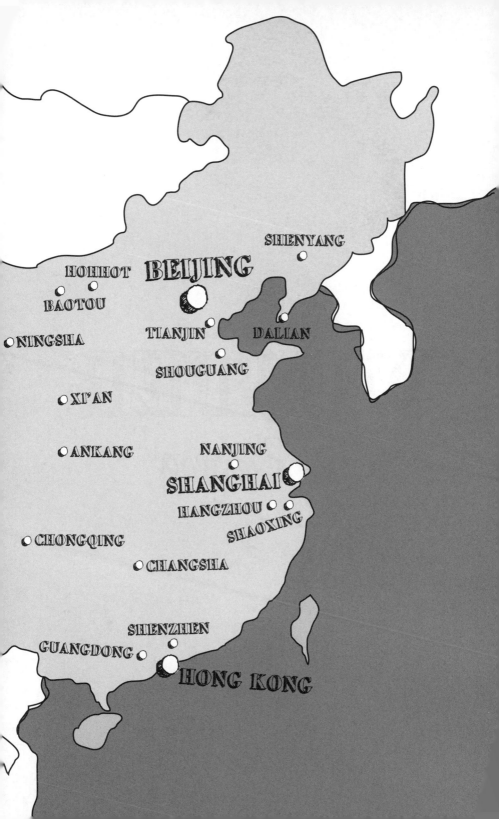

WINTER
in Beijing

The wind is cutting through the brightly coloured long coats, Parkas and quilted jackets that be-speckle the streets of Beijing. The temperature has dropped 10 degrees in the past two days and winter is here. The trees are being stripped of their leaves, which swirl everywhere, into coats and crannies and are trailed into public buildings, offices and homes alike. Ice flecks the pavements, some of it from the rather disgusting personal habit, of loudly clearing the throat followed by random spitting, that even known government displeasure seems to have failed to stamp out. You also have to watch out for restaurant spillages as you navigate the huddled pavements. But one blessing comes with the biting cold. It blows away the heavy layer of soot and carbon-filled haze that otherwise smothers the city like an unwelcome duvet on a hot summer night.

# Hungry for brands

I am accosted as I sit down after a long day of meetings and conference calls. I had hoped to retire to my coffee haven to regroup. The three women are in their mid-20s and keen to practise their English. Already married, one with a little girl at home with her own mother, they all work and are all clinging to their designer handbags as if they were babies.

The conversation starts with the usual Chinese quiz. "Who are you?" "What do you do?" "Where is your hometown?" "Why are you in China?" "How old are your children?" On both sides, the pleasantries then move from the mundane to a more interesting topic altogether: money.

One of the things that Chinese people have never really had much of is money, at least until very recently. Although the Chinese invented the stuff a couple of thousand years ago the masses never really experienced what it was like to have enough to do any more than survive. More recently, that has all changed. There are more than 300 million Chinese people said to be 'middle class' and this number is rising as prosperity, and a very Chinese brand of capitalism, takes hold. These girls are examples of this new found "emerging" middle class. Brand hungry, and with some money, they shop whenever they can, spending thoughtfully and sometimes lavishly.

Li has the classic Prada, Susan the latest Moschino and Lilly a last season Gucci.

"My husband thinks I'm mad," says Susan, when I comment about the bags and how expensive they must have been. Global brands don't drop their price in China, and in many instances, taxes and 'value pricing' ensures that the prices are appreciably higher than elsewhere in the world on these 'must have' items.

"I would never have been able to afford this unless I gave things up," says Li.

"Like what?"

"Like food!"

The story unfolds as the girls share the deliberate hardships they have chosen to endure in order to buy these statement goods. The notion of 'face' is well known in China, it revolves around showing and receiving respect and acknowledgement for, and from, others. For these girls, living in a society driven by increasing consumerism and material wealth, 'face' can be gained significantly by the ownership of high-quality and expensive goods. Possession shows or, more importantly, implies status, position and wealth. All these attributes are seen as important in raising you to a new level of stature and status among those around you. However, nowhere have I experienced it in such an extraordinary manner as with these girls. I learn that they are by no means alone and that thousands literally go without food to save enough money to buy certain items that give them huge 'face' with their family, friends and peers.

"Having the latest bag or shoes is really important," admits Lilly. "It shows how successful I have been, or how rich my husband is..." - though he isn't ... and Lilly is a secretary in a typing pool.

"There is another benefit to not eating so much," muses Li, "I can get into some lovely dresses too!"

As a Western man – or maybe just as a man – I struggle with the concept of giving up food for fashion, but cosmetics, accessories and luxury brands – especially foreign designer brands, are 'in' in a big way for the aspirant Chinese middle-class.

Lilly admits that, since she had her daughter a year ago, she has not been able to afford to buy anything new. But she has a baby, the other 'must have' fashion accessory for a young woman in China. Her mother looks after the child while she is at work, as most grandparents do in China. Lilly lives more than two hours' commute outside Beijing to the east, where house prices are lower. She still allows herself a once-a-month shop with friends, and often they stay over at each others' houses too so they can have a full "proper shopping day" in one or two of the major Beijing malls.

These young women are professional shoppers. Hours on the internet, swapping stories and experiences on Weibo and WeChat with friends and other like-minded value-seekers preceded the expedition to try on and review those revered goods. Buying white goods such as new refrigerators, air conditioners and the increasingly popular air filter to manage the Beijing pollution, is usually done during the national holidays (Golden Weeks) in October and Chinese New Year. Personal goods are bought as and when the girls have saved up enough, having gone without "less essential" things. But they're still looking for a bargain - they will always ask for a discount or seek out items that have an additional gift to go with them. Couple this with the benefit of mall discount cards and offers and somehow, through very rose-tinted spectacles from my perspective, it all seems worth the trouble!

Retailing and brand sales in China have to manage a very different psychology to the West. Those businesses that don't understand the psychology can get it very wrong indeed, but judging by the girls' unwavering focus, international fashion is going to run and run in China. Even as the top end is declining with the anti-corruption focus clamping down on high-cost gifts, the emerging middle- class in China is still demanding high-class fashion and foreign brands and will go to extraordinary lengths to possess them.

# Budget hotels and agility

David Sun had phoned me. It's typical of him not to be hierarchical. A short email had secured a direct call with the busy CEO of budget hotel chain Home Inns in China. David presides over a business with more than 250,000 beds per night to sell across 2,500 plus hotels in more than 300 Chinese cities. How many Western CEOs would call the personal mobile of someone they had only met three times in two years on the strength of a six-line email?

With David, who helped set up B&Q in China, small talk doesn't work, so I get straight to the point: "I heard you were in town for a few days, David. Are you free for a coffee in the next 72 hours?"

"Sure. Where are you?"

Typical of how things can occasionally move at lightning speed, and with amazing agility, in China, David is sitting in front of me just a few hours later.

I only gave him the English name of the coffee shop and the street. His driver then managed to negotiate the atrocious Beijing traffic to deposit him just outside the building only 10 minutes after the allotted time. Working to 'China time', that is nothing short of remarkable!

In China, there is an unspoken protocol for when to arrive for a meeting. It is considered rude to be late, much the same as in the UK or many Western cultures, but it is not seen as being rude to be up to 10 minutes early. My general rule of thumb is to manage arrival between five minutes early and up to 10 minutes late around any given time for a meeting. Traffic and other meetings over-running are acceptable reasons for additional lateness, but in Beijing and Shanghai, traffic often delays meetings for more than 20 minutes or even longer. Flexibility is essential here and planning more than a couple of important meetings in any one day is not advised.

The drinks are ordered as we walk in and we are soon deep in conversation. David barely draws breath for 30 minutes and still manages to drink a glass of water and two mugs of tea in the process. My coffee goes cold.

He is an effervescent, bullish and forthright leader with an infectious passion for his business, which he sees on a trajectory of continued expansion at up to 500 new hotels a year.

The transformation of China continues to impact every industry and the anti-corruption drive which started more than a year ago has been felt by the hotel and leisure industry as much as most. Cancelled events, reduced travel and gifting have rippled across the industry, to be felt even in the budget hotel market of Home Inns. However, David remains optimistic about the scope for growth in his sector. "This is the new normal," he says. "People and businesses should not overspend their budgets wherever they are." He feels that consumer habits are changing in terms of spending approach and there is more realism in spending with bookings focused on quality and value offerings rather than simply the luxury end of the market.

The market is full of competition. There are more than 10,000 branded budget hotels across China, and with the numbers rising, many are in the same cities as David's. The market is very fragmented and finding new opportunities and competitive locations is a problem. The scale of the country is his secret weapon. "We are now focused on opening in more of the third- and fourth-Tier cities and our franchise model allows us to be very flexible in the way we expand and where."

Benefiting from the invaluable knowledge of local entrepreneurs - and franchisees - helps mitigate the risk of new openings and new provincial city markets. David predicts that more than 85% of future openings will be under the franchise model. There remains the challenge of the Chinese holiday seasons when most people travel and occupancy is not a problem, but at other times, including midweek and away from the key holiday periods, hitting the numbers is tough, wherever you are across this vast and varied country. "We really need to leverage our position across the year," says David. There are also significant variations in site profitability from province to province. However, with China being bigger than Europe, with the regional variations that go with that, it is not surprising that disposable incomes, spending habits and attitudes to travel and hotel stays also vary significantly. Pricing strategies and wages do too.

This would sound horribly familiar to the likes of Premier Inn in the UK or any lower-cost hotel provider across the US or Europe. The comparisons don't stop there either. The challenge of getting the right, well trained, management and staff to run the sites is another continual concern for David. "The biggest challenge is human resources. It is increasingly difficult to find, hire, train and retain the right staff. We invest enormous effort, time and money in our people."

There is one noticeable difference between the conversation with David and his Western counterparts. The high-touch, always on, internet consumers in China are driving the business model far more, and far more quickly, than in Western markets. "The Chinese middle-classes are growing and they are in their 30s. They were in their mid-teenage years at the millennium when China really moved into the internet age. The late 20- and early-to-mid-30-year-olds are those entering the consumer segment with the majority of the spending power. These consumers are more independent, more active, more lifestyle- and self-orientated as well as enjoying more freedom and being more open to change than their parents and grandparents ever were." With this very savvy, web-based, consumer group at the heart of the business everything David talks about has an online aspect. From research to booking, payment and billing, online is everything and mobile solutions dominate. David and his team are spending a lot of time looking at creating offerings to develop and enhance consumer loyalty online and through mobile delivery.

"Is China the only market for Home Inns?" I ask. David is coy about answering. "There remains lots of room for movement in China. There is about 20% - 30% growth available to us in China. The growth opportunities elsewhere are perhaps 3% or 4%. However, we are open to the rest of South East Asia and to working with people in Europe and elsewhere. As Chinese consumers travel more and more, they will look for brands they know and can rely on. We can benefit from that development as the market opens up." Right now, David remains focused on China and listening to him talk it is clear why.

David leaves as speedily as he arrived. His driver has waited and braved the wrath of the local parking attendants and office security by double parking in the car park entrance – the hallowed no man's land between paying for a parking space and getting towed away by irate car park owners. He's clearly played this game before too.

*Insurance in China - luxury not necessity*

Alice Fan Yang steps elegantly into the coffee shop. It's been a year since we last met but she seamlessly picks up the conversation where we left off, such is the poise and professionalism of this successful and highly motivated Chinese businesswoman.

Alice is Assistant President at New China Asset Management (NCAM). She has responsibility for delivering a steady stream of sound investment deals to support the growing and ever-expanding commercial insurance arm.

We exchange pleasantries and the coffees are ordered. Educated in China, but with a wide experience of working outside, mainly on the west coast of the US, Alice speaks perfect English.

The conversation ranges from the choice of her daughter's next school (in Brighton or Windsor) to the complexities and challenges of the Chinese insurance market. On the important matter of her daughter's education we first swap notes on our own very different educational backgrounds and discuss the merits of the English school system versus that of the US. Alice wants her daughter to have as rounded an education as possible. Her preference is that her daughter has a private school education in the south of England. This will provide not only a solid academic grounding but access to the history and tradition of London as well as Paris and the continent (for family holidays). However, she also wants her to return to China thereafter to do a degree at one of the better Chinese universities. "It's important that she has a world view but also that she comes back to help our country succeed and to benefit from the success as well. She has had a good start with the Chinese system but now, since we can afford it, my husband and I want her to get a different perspective on life and the world before coming back to China."

"So, how's work?" I ask casually.

Alice sips her cappuccino, smiles gently at me and settles into her chair. She then, smoothly and faultlessly, outlines the challenges of succeeding in the fast-developing and increasingly volatile market of the Chinese insurance sector.

"There has been significant change in the market over the past 12-18 months," says Alice. "The whole asset management sector has become much more market-orientated. The rebalancing of the Chinese economy and the speed of change has meant many investment products have failed to launch. Just a year ago, there were good asset-based investment opportunities in real estate but these have evaporated in the wake of the well-publicized over-supply in that sector."

"Interest rates are now much more market-driven than in 2013, as the central government has allowed market forces to rebalance the economy and markets generally. This has created problems for all industries, but the significant fluctuations in interest rate returns from investments has made many investors think twice about putting their money into certain types of assets. Infrastructure remains the most attractive option," reflects Alice. "New airports, roads, rail and port developments have been seen as much safer bets than the corporate or private housing real estate market which is not only suffering from over-supply but also very low returns."

"There are more products in the market than ever before. Investors have more choice than ever before and this has not ever been seen in China until recently. The offerings have moved from being relatively simple and straight forward to highly complex, sophisticated and often mixed in their composition."

Alice believes these changes are also leading to product offerings which are increasingly tailor-made to specific investors. "I am spending most of my time directly connecting with the key potential investor," she says. "This is really to understand better what they want, what their investment appetite is and how we can satisfy that while managing our risk effectively. It is a tough market and a tough job!"

Alice tells me that the whole of the asset management market has also changed in the past year as the Chinese government has introduced measures to eliminate the middlemen in the asset investment game. "It used to be that we would sell in to trusts but that pushed up costs to the end investor - including government," says Alice. My understanding of the situation she described is that this meant returns for the real investors were reduced. That was alright up to a point in the big growth years when margins were good, but now they are not. Now the government, understandably, wants better returns to be passed on to all investors and the squeeze is on the trusts and other intermediaries. That in turn means organizations such as Alice's have had to totally change their market and customer focus.

"We are looking at truly sustainable investments on a much longer term return basis," continues Alice. "This is changing the dynamic of the asset investment and the way we can package deals to investors, which, in turn, affects how the sales teams can make offers to consumers and commercial insurance buyers."

I have personally learned that the Chinese insurance market is quite different to elsewhere in the world as the end consumers expect that the money, which, as customers they are tying up in premiums, is also giving them something back as an investment. "If you are trying to give end consumers a 6% return on their premium, then you had better make sure you are getting at least 8% on your asset investment return," says Alice.

Alice tells me that this need to find high yields for end consumers puts pressure on finding sustainable and lower-risk investments, as well as accessing those investors who are prepared to take the risk that goes with the high returns. "Somewhere along the line you have to take a very cool view of the risk profile of every potential deal," Alice comments. "That's my job, to ensure the risk reward balance is there and that the asset really can deliver the returns which people demand. Sometimes it just is not possible but we have to manage the risk so we don't get defaults and failures."

"Real estate used to be a good bet, but the days when a developer could build and not worry about the management of the physical shopping mall or commercial site are gone. The whole market is rebalancing and developers have to have a strong customer focus and to have done the numbers, as well as the market research, to ensure the market is really there and can sustain the sales, which sustains the rental, which delivers the return on investment of the site".

"The game has fundamentally changed," says Alice. "The investors are also faced with myriad different products, many of which only have small differences between them. They need to be much more sophisticated in their assessment of what they are buying."

With little to differentiate offers, or the offers being highly complex, investors are having to make decisions as much about the asset management company and its brand as the apparent attractiveness of the deal. This is where Alice believes NCAM has an edge. "We may be smaller than others but we have a good brand and a track record for delivering consistent returns."

Many investors still trust in the decisions of government, either at a central or provincial level. They tend to follow the provincial government lead. However, there have been defaults and failures, so investors are wary of those regions with a bumpy track record. "Provincial government are brands too," explains Alice, "and where there have been highly publicized problems, then investors tend to be super-cautious, preferring to look elsewhere for a safe harbour for their money."

Alice reminds me that when a consumer insurance offer looks too good to be true, it probably is. "There are a lot of aggressive product sales out there, even being offered on Taobao," she says, referring to the widely used internet search engine of China. She believes this is a move destined to failure and investor disappointment: "Deals may look good, but high returns in this market inevitably mean high-risk asset investments somewhere along the line." Several companies have had the regulators issue warnings and more are likely to come if the aggressive sales and seemingly high returns bubble bursts. That will not be good for anyone in this new and emerging market.

Alice feels some of the market deals are very creative and could be attractive to many. Her only concern is the transparency of the associated risk. "Of course, if investors are happy to take the risk for a high return, that's fine," she says, "but I believe that there must be transparency and a full disclosure to the end investor of the risk level of the high return deals." Listening to Alice, you are reminded that this industry is in its infancy and, as such, it is undergoing enormous change. The expectations of the end consumer are high and the pressure on the assets investment business significant. Only time will tell how this industry survives the pressure of the rebalancing of China.

Alice leaves as elegantly as she arrived, her designer shoes barely clicking as she walks across the wooden floor. She even pays for our coffees, despite me offering the obligatory three times. "Buy me dinner next time we meet," she says quietly, as we walk out. "Perhaps we could invite some others?" she almost throws the remark away as she parts. "Great!" I mirror her almost imperceptible enthusiasm. "That would be lovely."

Even in this small exchange there is great meaning. Alice has accepted me as an appropriate acquaintance and is prepared to open up her world to me slowly through the time-honoured Chinese route of shared food and private conversation.

The lesson here? After a personal introduction through a mutual friend and two meetings, a year apart, the relationship with Alice has moved from pure business to potential dinner guest. Relationships are everything in China and you respect them above everything else, or you fail. Time for a beer…

# There is no chapter four

My colleague screwed up her nose.

"I really wouldn't do that."

"Do what?" I stopped in mid-flow of my explanation to the bank clerk that I wanted to transfer £250 from my international account to my local Chinese one.

"Don't transfer £250."

I wasn't aware she had been listening to my discussion about a personal transaction but I let that pass in my curiosity.

"Why not?'"

"It's a bad number."

Some swift-but-delicate quizzing (with an eye to the grumpiness of the next customer in line) was worthwhile.

The Chinese are superstitious when it comes to numbers. Indeed, they are superstitious about many things. Portents, omens and auspicious happenings have been part of Chinese history and culture for thousands of years. There are books written on the subject. It should be taken very seriously indeed by anyone wishing to understand the Chinese and their culture better.

Numbers are important to the Chinese and readers interested in this subject should do their research carefully. Having an important meeting or event on the 'wrong' date can result in no one showing up. I have now got used to asking "what date would be best for you?" or "is there a better date for this meeting, event or activity?" It is always appreciated, and the choice of a good date, driven by the lunar calendar and not the Western one, will result in smiles and satisfaction. Deals can be won and lost on the signing date being a 'good' or a 'bad' one. In addition, arranging meetings or visits around the major holidays is a disaster. Avoid the times immediately before and after Chinese New Year, Lantern Festival, Mid-Autumn Festival and Labour Day at the very least. All of these, except Labour Day, which is always on 1 May, are governed by the lunar calendar so the Western date changes every year.

The lunar calendar governs much of the Chinese annual cycle and indeed the cycle of life in China. Watch out for birthdays. Since the Chinese use the lunar calendar, don't assume that your friends' or colleagues' birthdays will be on the same Western date each year. They won't be. Most Chinese people working with foreigners opt for a standard birthday date for ease, but they will still celebrate the right birthday date, according to the lunar calendar, with friends and family.

Equally important are phrases and gifts. Weddings, in particular, and certain other events where money is often the main gift, are fraught with numerical complications. The number eight is a good number and 888 is a great one. Apartments in high rise developments on floors eight or 18 or 28 will be much more expensive.

Back in the bank, my colleague explained that when 250 is said in the Chinese language, it sounds very similar to the characters for 'imbecile'. The counter staff were now giggling almost uncontrollably. Rather sheepishly, I amended my transfer to a less 'stupid' number and everyone dissolved into smiles of cross-cultural understanding.

So, I have found to my cost that numbers are important. So important, indeed, that since the sound of the character for the number four is very similar to the sound of the character for death, you will not find a fourth floor button in lifts, there will be no block four in housing estates, no row four or seat four in cinemas and no fourth chapter in this book.

# The Journalist

Yang Yang (not his real name) is a journalist for a financial paper in China. A confident 25-year-old, he nevertheless does not want to be quoted officially. He is, however, happy to talk, via the gauze of partial anonymity and is content that his photograph will not be enough to single him out.

Yang is still studying journalism at one of the Beijing universities. He has just had exams and is not confident of having done well.

"I earn my living as a full-time journalist, so I have to do all my study in my spare time," he says. "I am lucky since my job means I have quite a lot of flexibility, so I have been able to work my studies into my schedule, though sometimes it is very difficult."

His round face and complexion single him out to the trained eye as being from one of the many minorities in China. He hails from Xiang Cheng, a town in Hunan Province in northern China, where his parents are farmers.

"They are simple people and have a simple and quite an easy life. My father is a carpenter, so during the famines he still can work and earn enough money to survive."

The famines occur each year between June and September, when the earth is parched by the dry and arid winds from the Northern Steppes and wilder Mongolian plains. His parents, he tells me, have little education but supported him to have one. He managed to pass the exams to get to University in Nanjing in Southern China to study international audit but dropped out after a year.

"I found it was not for me," he explains." I just left and went back home to my parents and back to high school for another two years so I could retake the entrance exams. I was lucky. I worked hard and got to this course in Beijing. My parents could not help me. They didn't understand what or why I was doing what I was doing. I just had to struggle on my own. My parents let me decide everything about my life myself. They could see how ambitious I was and just tried hard to support my decisions. I have a good relationship with my parents but I don't have much time to be able to spend with them. I only go home once a year at Spring Festival for a couple of weeks. I really have nothing in common with the people in my home town. My old friends there are married with kids and have simple, easy jobs in the factories or working for the government. They don't understand why I am not married with children. I am ambitious and I want to be able to grab the opportunities of the new China. I have new friends here in Beijing."

The coffee in front of him grows cold. I bought it without thinking. He sips it occasionally. He only drinks tea.

He interviews me too. But not about business. About life, places I have been, people met, stories shared, experiences of China, family, friends and food. It is an easy conversation.

"I never can talk to my parents like this." His dark eyes seem large behind his equally large glasses. "It is so different. Normally, I interview business people but they don't talk about their lives, the struggle they had or anything. It is just the bullshit of success and business. We have to write what is right for them or we get into trouble when they complain to the editor. They never share their real story. It is difficult.

"When I was young, I was ambitious, it was in my heart, it still is, I don't know why. I always wanted to better myself, not to just survive but to be successful. Right now, I just have to survive. I have no choice. But I will be successful."

We discuss what 'success' means. It has a very different shape and tone to the definition found outside China in the West.

"For the Chinese, owning a house means everything. It means stability; it means security. When men from the country go away to the big cities, often they will do low-wage jobs. However, they will still save and save as much as they can. They will eat little and simply, they will sleep in cheap places. Usually their employer provides basic dormitory accommodation and food for the workers, sometimes actually on the construction site. Everything they save will go home to their wife and children to look after them. But more than that, they will be trying to earn enough money to buy some small bit of land and to build a house. To them, that is success, so their children will have a house to live in."

There is a whole sub-class of migrant workers who are the hands behind the infrastructure developments driving much of China's economic growth. These workers leave family behind for up to a year at a time, commuting home, often taking days to do so, for the national holiday of Chinese New Year. The way these workers are paid, or not paid, is little appreciated outside China. Most do not receive any money at all until the company for which they work receives their payments at the different stages of a development's completion. In some cases, workers are not paid until Chinese New Year each year. Back home, families struggle to survive until the annual wage arrives, often physically with the worker. Newspapers and the internet report stories of workers who have not been paid for more than a year and unscrupulous contractors who fail to pay at all. In a couple of cases, reports emerged recently of children and impoverished wives committing suicide to draw attention to the plight of their migrant fathers and spouses, unpaid for a year and then told to sue for their wages.

I ask Yang for his definition of success:

"Of course, I send money back to my parents but my mother just saves it. She says they have enough with their simple lives and she will have it all to give me when I get married so I can buy a house. They give up everything for this common dream of Chinese parents for their children. Success, for me, is to be able to work in finance. My main degree is in journalism but my passion is economics and finance. I hope maybe in five years' time I will be a manager in a finance company. My real dream is to have my own business.

"I am ambitious because of my past. I had a difficult time, I had to struggle to get my exams and then it was a big decision to drop out of Nanjing and start again. I have had to really overcome many difficulties in my life."

As Yang talks, he becomes more animated and his voice trembles a little as he sketches out the dreams of obtaining a Master's degree, travelling and being his own boss.

"I said, a year ago, that perhaps I would go to do a Master's degree in Canada, the US, or the UK, but now I have changed my mind," he says. "Partly because it would cost me so much money but also because China has changed and there are more opportunities I can see here. So I hope I can do a Master's perhaps in Singapore or Hong Kong or Shanghai. My first choice would now be Shanghai, then Singapore and Hong Kong last." We pause for a moment as he reflects on what he has said.

"I do not see Hong Kong as the gateway of finance to China any more. It used to be, but I can see the change happening. Shanghai is important and all the policies (government) are supporting the development of Chinese finance, insurance and capital markets. Working in financial journalism, I am seeing the regulations changing almost every year and there are new ones which will also make a big change. It is happening. China is growing and developing fast.

"The world position of China is changing. I can see the effects of this every day in my job. China is expanding everywhere."

Watching the daily news broadcasts, I could be persuaded to believe this too, through the crafted scripts, but Yang is on the inside and his is another perspective, truer perhaps?

"The reforms and changes may seem slow to the West but one or two years in China are fast and if you join up all the dots of the past 10 years you can see the direction changing and it is clear."

I am reminded that the Chinese don't plan for the short term (at least, not for tomorrow or next week), but they do plan for the next 50 or even 100 years. In that context, the changes may seem slow to the untutored eye but to those living in it every day they can feel the tilt of change as the wind shifts East.

"My daily life is not affected by the movement of China in the world, but my future is."

There is a profundity in this simple statement from the 25-year-old man before me.

Doubtless, he is one of the emerging urban middle class of China. "I have just enough money to live my life ok," he says. But he is also one of the many younger rising educated and ambitious generation that is the backbone of the future success of China in the world. There is a rawness of determination to succeed that is to be found across China but in Beijing and some of the other bigger Tier 1 and Tier 2 cities; you can almost feel it around you in the coffee shops and middle-income eateries. Here, earnest conversations can be overheard planning business, doing deals and dreaming of success. The smartphones buzz incessantly during the lunch break and early evening food times. Groups bent over tablets and laptops tap out the future. There is business to be done out there and there are risks worth taking to share in the China Dream.

What are Yang's thoughts on Western society?

"People have an easier life in the West. The Western culture is much more mature than in China. Here, people still have to struggle and work hard all the time. I am just one of those people. But things are changing for the better here. We have many problems and challenges, but although life is hard, it is getting better slowly. In the West, life is simple and easy."

I am intrigued by his perspective, and after some encouragement, Yang explains his views in more detail:

"I believe that Western people have an easier life. It is just my feeling. The ratio between house prices (back to that focus of importance) and wages in the West is much narrower than here in China. Here, it is just so big it is almost impossible to bridge without the help of family. In the West, insurance gives you security, but here we don't have that type of luxury. It is the security of a house that matters. The living expenses in the West are also lower than here if you compare the ratio of wages to prices. Here, prices are going up and up and wages are not. China is also a cash society. We don't do debt! If we need cash, we will borrow from family first. In the West, the attitude to security and the attitude to life is very different to here."

Yang sits back, seemingly exhausted by the enormity of it all.

"Western people want an easy life, but in China no one has an easy life. So we just have to work hard to earn a living and struggle to build our own security."

We share a long silence. There is not much to say. The chasm of culture and dreams is too great. I endeavour to bring the conversation back home.

What of his extended family?

"I have two older brothers, one is in my home town but the other is in Shanghai. We do not connect often – except, of course, at Spring festival." No more is said. Silence descends again between us like a shroud. The family matter is a closed door. It is his past and not his future. Yang has all the enthusiasm of youth but there is no naivety. His life has already been too hard, too difficult, to remain naive. He has a girlfriend, also 25, who recently graduated with a degree in English.

Will he get married and have children? "Perhaps, one day, but not yet. I am ambitious and I want to grab the opportunities that I can see and dream of. She is not ambitious. She wants a more simple life."

Poor girl.

"Maybe in five years' time you and I will meet in London where I will be on business and I can tell you about my success," he concludes.

There is no hint of irony or the rose-tinted passion of a dreamer. It is simply a statement of fact. He will be successful, he will share in the wider prosperity of China in the world and he will make his parents proud of him.

# The Welsh, Chinese oil man

Ling Lai is a Hong Kong-born business executive, raised in Wales and now working for a Chinese-owned, Australia-based, oil company, while living in Beijing. He is a devout and practising Christian.

"I have to say that I struggled with my identity when I first arrived in the country in 1995," he admits. "I felt I had landed on a different planet. It was a real journey of self-discovery. I was working for BP as a project manager in those days, and having joined in the UK, I was then sent to China about 1,000 miles up the Yangtze river into Chongqing in Sichuan Province, to build an acid plant. It was one of the first joint ventures in the petroleum industry between China and the West."

Ling spent almost three years commuting each day across a region of precipitous mountain passes with almost impassable and hair-raising roads. His guest house was spartan and uninviting. To make things even more challenging he had to manage a workforce of almost 10,000 locals.

"It used to take anything up to two hours on a good day and could be an all-night stress run on sheet ice in the winter. Today, it takes about 30 minutes on the expressway since they sliced through the mountains a few years ago."

Such is the pace of change in China, and the investment in infrastructure, that the old ways have disappeared under the concrete and asphalt of progress.

Ling continued to search for his identity, caught between his Western upbringing but Chinese roots, with a family originally from Guangdong. "The danger of being in the middle of the road is that you get run over." He smiles gently. "It's taken me 18 years to feel comfortable in my own skin here. I love this country. I am Chinese racially but can never be truly Chinese. People often call me a banana, yellow on the outside, white on the inside." It's a common reference to the overseas second or third generation returnees to China. They are never quite Chinese by birth and not quite Western by experience.

"I have stopped worrying about it." Ling's soft and somewhat disarming smile appears again. "I am who I am. I can't help it, I do have a Western perspective, an international perspective. When I arrived, I had a somewhat misguided and romantic view of China based on my Western upbringing and education. I came down to earth with a bump!

"The accounting and finance office was still using the abacus and rice paper vouchers. But two years later, we had an effective, bilingual, fully integrated ERP system that could be accessed from head office in London, 24 hours-a-day. It was so impressive how fast people learned and absorbed things. The Chinese people had, and have, an incredible capacity to absorb, assess, learn and execute new ideas and approaches. They make them their own, they make them Chinese and there is a hunger for self-betterment and to better people's lives which I just never see in the West."

Ling met his wife in Sichuan and they married in 2003. Now living permanently in Beijing, they return to the UK to visit family as often as they can. She is the head of human resources for a large Chinese corporate, headquartered in Beijing.

"It was my wife who introduced me to Christianity," continues Ling. She was already a member of the church, and when we moved to Beijing in 2005, she wanted to attend the international church here. Of course, I loved her very much so agreed to tag along. It was strange showing your passport at the door to get into the church but that's how it is here."

Ling displays his faith easily and gently. "Man plans the steps, but God has the final say," he sums up. "I was lucky to be sent to Harvard Business School by BP in 2005 and that increased my hunger to learn more about both the world and myself. It also further activated my curiosity about the church and Christ. I became a Christian in November 2006 on my return from the US."

Religion has had a long tradition in China with Buddhism being more than 1,000 years old in the country. Other beliefs, Taoism in particular, are referenced in Chinese classical literature such as The Romance of the Three Kingdoms (San Guo Yan Yi). It's China's oldest novel thought to have been compiled by a 14th century poet, Lo Guanzhong. An epic of blood, brotherhood, treachery and loyalty, it's at the heart of classical Chinese culture, as are its central characters including a revered monk-turned-political strategist.

Ling's experience in the oil industry charts the changes in China's energy business.

"In the early days, it was all about using the Chinese labour and supply chain to transfer technology and experience from the West into China. Then, between 2006 and 2010, I noticed a real shift in emphasis. The game got significantly bigger and more commercial. The Chinese energy companies ceased to be shy about where they went in the world to source energy and reserves. Not everyone agreed with their move into Africa and the Middle East, but from 2010, they really started to compete on the global stage much more effectively. They were using their labour, supply chain, political and commercial skill and know-how to leverage their position."

In 2010, Ling found himself sitting in the middle of an Iraqi desert with Chinese riggers and drillers leading a joint venture project with BP, Sinopec and the Iraqis.

"In 2001, I would never have believed I could ever be part of China's overseas oil exploration. It would have been unimaginable a few years before, when China was really focused on internal affairs and not overseas. It shows how far China has come in such a short time, from domestically focused development to taking to the world stage."

The project was one of the early successes of the expansion overseas of China's energy business and has been followed by many more ventures all over the world, as the country's energy industry goes further and further afield in search of the natural resources the super power needs to sustain its economic growth and development.

Now working for an Australian company owned by a Chinese asset management business, which also owns interests in German and Portuguese enterprises, Ling is in the middle of the new China ownership and stakeholding model.

"It's a sign of the times and of the emerged powerhouse of China," He says. That smile again. "I am very comfortable with it. It seems a natural move in the greater scheme of things. China has gone global and there is no stopping it. You can feel it and experience it changing around you. It is one of the wonderful things about working here."

I ask Ling if he sees this changed China in the values of its people. "Are those changing too?"

"No. I think it is still about self-improvement, about face and about family. These are core to Chinese thinking, and while the pace of change picks up, I see these staying the same. With the focus on family, and pleasing mum and dad by being successful, there are emerging tensions and stresses. Some of these exist between the young who want to embrace the new opportunities and the older generation who venerate the past, and the struggle to get China to where it is now, but things are changing."

So, I question Ling directly, is he still searching for his identity?

"Not any longer." Again that smile. "China has changed me and moulded me considerably, good and bad, personally and professionally. It has been a part of me for so long and I am nothing but thankful for it. My faith has grown and that too has shaped and helped me develop. But above all, China helped me grow up."

# The man who met the Queen

Jeffery was born in 1982 in west Beijing. He is a Beijinger. Recently married and living in his own apartment immediately above that of his parents, he is typical of his generation of well-educated, middle class Chinese. Schooled first in a local kindergarten and junior school, his parents managed to get him into a Canadian school in Beijing. One of the burgeoning international schools in China, the school gave him the international education his parents wanted for their son. Later, he was sent to the UK to complete his A-levels at Broxtowe College, Nottinghamshire followed by Keele University, where he read Economics and Business Administration between 2001 and 2004.

"I sort of see myself as being a little bit British," he says. "I spent so long there, it is almost like a second home to me. I loved it there. I was lucky, because when I finished university, I went to London to train in accounting to get an Association of Chartered Certified Accountants qualification as a part-time student. I was so lucky. I lived in the centre of London in Warren Street for 18 months. My parents served in the military, but a long time ago, and they returned to Beijing in the 1980s. My father was involved in the set up of the Beijing Stock Exchange. My mother worked at the Beijing Bureau of Finance. They are both retired now."

I ask Jeffery why he decided to return to China.

"I wanted to come back. There is so much opportunity here. I set up a business with a friend in Changsha. We had a marketing and advertising agency for two years. He had lots of contacts with the local government and we did ok for a while. However, it was hard and we decided to close it after two years and I came back to Beijing. I got a job with one of the emerging accounting and finance firms here and have been working there ever since. We are now much more international and it is really interesting to see how the business has developed over the years. It's a bit weird sometimes as we are a local company, and very Chinese in management style."

Jeffery sees one overarching difference between the traditional Chinese business and that of the West.

"It is really significant. Traditional Chinese companies are very hierarchical. The boss is really the boss and the workers are the workers and pretty well do as they are told. I work in marketing and it is different as we have a more internationally-minded manager, but it is a struggle sometimes. Though it is much better than it used to be. When we were a really, totally local business we were working all hours and weekends, it was so tough and we just had our heads down all the time with a small team. Now, we have a much better way of working with a lot more flexibility. I usually leave at 18.00 so there is time for me to get home and spend time with my new wife and to see my parents. I now can see my parents every day for at least half-an-hour a day."

I was fortunate enough to have attended Jeffery's wedding last year, and it seemed appropriate to explore his views on marriage as a relatively newlywed.

"My wife comes from Shen Yang in Liaoning province. A friend of mine introduced us. She works in Beijing. We met in February 2012 and got married in October 2014. We are a good match. I really view marriage very seriously indeed. Not everyone does, you know."

Reflecting on his comments, I am reminded of the many stories from friends and acquaintances of couples marrying for convenience and security, rather than love.

"I think it is a huge responsibility," he says. "You have to be willing to spend the rest of your life with the other person. I must admit that I was a little scared and fearful of getting married. But I overcame my fear since our personalities are so well-matched. We are very balanced together. She is not materialistic either so we have a good shared set of values. I knew she was the one from very early on in our relationship. We hope to have children next year, perhaps. We are a little unusual in China as a young couple as we live separately from both our parents. We have been able to buy our own place in the same block as my parents, so we are close but also separate. It is a perfect way of living."

Our conversation turns to the subject of 'sheng nv'. This is the Chinese name for a group of women in their 30s who are single. Directly translated it means "the women who are left behind". In China, it is estimated that by the year 2020 there will be around 30 million more men than women between the ages of 25 and 40, mainly in the rural areas. The reality is that in the cities there are more single women. This goes deep into the Chinese culture. In the rural areas, the pressure to have boys as the single child has led, one way or another, to there being more boys than girls. This pressure historically stemmed from the need for a secure source of labour and income for the future of the family. Stories of infanticide still circulate across China and there is too much 'noise in the system' to ignore it. Unwanted pregnancies in girls under the age of 18 was a factor in the past. The costs and social stigma of fatherless children didn't help either. Certainly, the facts are that women find it easier to live in the cities. More freedom is certainly a factor, and away from the rural pressure to marry and conform, they are either choosing to marry later or simply can't find the right urban partner with the same 'new' attitudes. These girls are in a rush to get married. Their biological clocks are ticking but their attitudes and urbanized freedoms of jobs and money hold them back.

"In the second Tier cities girls tend to get married before they are 25 years old. In the really rural communities, women will get married in their early 20s. Parents want girls to marry early so they will have grandchildren in time to look after them in their old age. In the big cities, people are more open-minded and see the whole matter of marriage as not just the parents' decision. Also, when these 'sheng nv' look for a husband, they will look above to an older man, even a man who might be divorced. The older men look for a younger woman so there is a match but the sheng nv don't really have much choice. In the big cities like Beijing and Shanghai the majority of parents expect their daughter to find someone who has a house. They will be much more supportive of their daughter dating a man who owns a house than with someone who doesn't."

There is a question I have long been wary of asking people I have met in China, but the conversation seems to allow it here. "Does love matter in marriage?"

Jeffery pauses for a long time.

"Well. Even if a couple is in love they will be under a lot of pressure. Some just don't get married or have to marry someone they don't love because the parents will not agree to them marrying the person they do love. The pressures are very high, from parents, friends, work and even society."

I recently heard of a landlord refusing to take a single girl as a tenant unless they could speak to the girl's parents to establish their support for her as single and of good repute. In another instance, I have heard of women being overlooked in promotion at work in certain Chinese companies as they were seen as immature, and not ready for responsibility, as they weren't married and did not have a child.

"In Beijing it is definitely the tradition that the guy provides a house for the marriage. The girl will provide the car. I know it is a bit materialistic, but it is a financial guarantee for a good marriage and a better future. It's very common. In the largest cities, there are fewer men who own a house than those who don't among the ages of 20 and 30, the prime years for marriage. In big cities such as Beijing and Shanghai, buying a house is a precondition of getting married. Both families will put all they can, all their savings, into a house for the couple. There is a philosophy about houses. It is the most important thing to a Chinese person. Without a house, you don't have a home! No home and you have no family! It means security. It is seen as very bad to live in someone else's house, like a rented place. It isn't good. You need to own your own place. My parents spent their lives saving for me and my wife and I will spend our lives saving for our children. It's the Chinese way."

The Chinese save money. The facts have been recounted elsewhere in these notes. Chinese people will save almost 50% of their salary each year, where Westerners will be lucky to save almost 12%.

"Chinese tourists spent ¥6bn in 10 days in Japan over this year's Chinese New Year. We have money and we are prepared to spend it. Before the Chinese travelled abroad as we do now, no one knew about this aspect of our culture. Now they do. I hear that 12% of buildings bought in Australia in 2014 were sold to Chinese!"

I know this personally. A friend of mine who lives in Australia is selling his house and advertising it on Chinese websites. He has been advised to search for buyers in China, as Australians are less likely to be able to afford the high price tag on his beautiful and secluded home than wealthy Chinese people with an eye to emigration. He is even contemplating attending sales events in Beijing organized by enterprising real estate middle men.

Somehow, our conversation ranges from topic to topic around money until we settle on a personal favourite. Banks. And service. Or the lack of it.

"Banks don't care and they don't put customer service high on their list of priorities," asserts Jeffery. "The big banks are state-owned. They are just too big. They are among the biggest banks in the world, let alone in China. ICBC is the biggest in the world, Bank of China is huge too and they get too much money from business to bother about their private customers. Add to that, the restrictions on foreign banks in China, and there is no motivation to improve service at all, there is just no big competition."

The waiting times in China's banks are legendary. The seeming slickness of the electronic ticketing and queuing system belies the true crushing inefficiency. Chronically understaffed branches are the norm, with those staff that are there generally diffident, uninterested and ponderous. The systems are slow and tedious with the procedures and processes, bureaucratic and arcane. Add to this 'random' security scrutiny and senior-level oversight and you have a recipe for utter customer disservice. It is an ominous clue of what awaits the inexperienced or virgin customer that most branches have a 'customer waiting area', usually of some considerable size, with uncomfortable chairs.

It is not uncommon for people to wait an hour for relatively simple transactions, like getting a bank statement printed, which took me a full 45 minutes last week, in an empty bank branch. Resident Chinese people, on the other hand, can expect to wait two-to-three hours if they want to do a relatively complex transaction, such as currency exchange between two accounts. This sort of 'specialist' banking usually only has one staff member allocated to it and often, in central Beijing at least, several customers waiting at any one time.

Jeffery continues: "Banks that are smaller offer better service as they know that they have to compete. So ones like China Merchant Bank or Minsheng Bank are a lot better on service."

Not surprisingly, there has been a quantum leap in online banking. In digital China, there are more and more mobile banking applications available to do all the things the West is increasingly taking for granted and several innovations which are yet to hit many 'developed' countries' service providers. You can do pretty much anything you like online if you have money, certainly if it involves depositing it in large quantities. Actually, most ATM machines have a deposit facility and you do see many Chinese people with wads of cash in everything from brown paper bags (yes really) to smart security satchels, feeding the distinctive red ¥100 notes into hungry machines.

The issue is big withdrawals. Even transfers from one account to another in your own name. That is always a trial.

"I am really lucky since I have spare cash, I own my house so have no mortgage," says Jeffery. "My wife and I have more leisure time too so we spend it with friends, drinking and having food together, we go shopping, to the movies and, of course, time with my parents."

These words are from the heart of the Chinese middle classes. Money to spend and the time to spend it. Priorities of family and the proximity to be able to achieve these priorities.

"I spend time with my parents every day. We will expect our children to look after us when we are old, and I am doing that for my parents now. It's the Chinese way. My wife goes back to visit her parents regularly too. She went back at Chinese New Year to be with her parents. It's so important. They are so important to both of us. Her parents are older now. Her father has a business selling heavy machinery to construction companies. It is getting harder and harder to make a sale as the real estate market has collapsed across China. It is really tough now. I think he will sell the business soon or just stop. It's just getting too hard to make it all work."

How does Jeffery feel about the prospects for China and himself as the country goes through a time of rebalancing and lower, though still reasonable, growth?

"I think I am normal among my peer group. I have no rent so I can spend my money on what I want to spend it on. Average salaries in Beijing are around ¥6000 - ¥7000 (£650 - £750) a month so it is really hard for those who do not have a house. Most people will have to spend over 50% of their monthly salary on their rent and the rest easily goes on food, so there is nothing left each month to put into saving for a house. And houses are expensive here. An average small house will cost about ¥30,000 (£3,300) per square metre. Mine was about ¥60,000 (£6,600)a square meter as we are near the second west ring road in central Beijing."

House prices in Beijing and in Shanghai are holding up. Indeed, they have increased even though elsewhere across China real estate prices and construction have collapsed, leaving great holes in the ground and the economy. I continue to see block after block of built and half-built residential blocks standing empty, but the cement and steel keeps being produced, the marble quarried and the migrant workers employed as the economy strides along seemingly impervious to the chronic over-supply and consequent potential social and infrastructure problems this is going to create.

Jeffery is contemplating his future and that of his children.

"We hope to have children next year and we are applying for Canadian citizenship for our unborn child."

This is news to me.

"My wife wants to live abroad and it is also for our children, we always wanted them to be able to be born abroad. My parents are ok with it. The pollution is just so bad in Beijing. It is a real issue. There are also the food safety hazards, the contamination of rice and basic foodstuffs is well known, from cooking oils to baby milk, we have to think about the health of our babies. If you want the highest standards of quality, mainly Western goods and products, then it is very expensive to get in Beijing. Overseas, where quality is a given in the food chain, there is more reliability. There is also our children's education. It is now a realistic choice for middle-class Chinese parents, to have their children educated abroad."

I ask him how long he would go for and whether he plans to return to China.

"Of course!" he replies. "It would only be for a few years while our children grow up and are schooled. Then, of course, we would come back. We haven't really thought about it. Staying away isn't really an option. My wife wants our baby to be born in Canada. It is one of the easier places for Chinese people to get citizenship. (Canada has just followed the US in agreeing to issue 10-year visas with China.) It is a big burden on my shoulders but we know the Chinese way is that if you give your best to your children then they will give their best to you as you grow old. My parents paid for me to go to school, it's a cycle of life so I will do the same for my children and look after my parents. It is what has happened generation after generation in China and will always be the way here. We all believe in the China Dream, that China will rise again, peacefully."

The paranoia of many Westerners regarding China should be assuaged by comments such as these from Jeffery, and so many of his middle-class cohorts. "The Chinese are happy being Chinese. We don't have imperialism or empire-building in our blood, like some other nations maybe (Jeffery winks at me).

To the Western mind, this may be seen as an odd comment to make. However, Chinese students are taught, from an early age, of the aggression and imperialist intentions of other nations, including Japan, the US and the UK. Western education of Chinese history will skim over much of the history which is taught in China. All the Chinese people I know have a significant grasp of every date and story associated with the history of the Boxer rebellion of 1899 – 1901 as well as the Japanese invasion of northern China in 1931 and atrocities in Nanjing by the Japanese in 1937. Readers wanting to understand more of the attitudes of the Chinese to current events should read widely on Chinese history. There is no substitute for deepening awareness and even a small amount of knowledge will be appreciated.

I avoid the temptation to repeat the earlier conversation about food and air quality. The irony isn't lost on Jeffery.

"I know it seems inconsistent to the Western mind, but we Chinese can hold conflicting ideas in our heads at the same time and be comfortable with them both. It is a cost of progress that we have to suffer now but it won't last for ever. We will manage things over time so the difficulties will be solved."

Jeffery fishes his smartphone from inside his jacket. After a quick search he shows me a digitized photograph from long ago. A fresh-faced and cherubic young boy in a group of kindergarten children.

"I wanted to show you this, I hope it is interesting," He says.

"It is," I reply.

"I met your queen."

"Really!?"

"Really. She came to Beijing in October 1986 on her first official visit. I was only four years old and don't really remember, but our kindergarten was chosen by the government to be visited as it was the best in Beijing at that time. Actually, it is still seen as the best. That was the reason I decided to go to study in the UK, to sort of pay the visit back. I love London, it is such an historic city, you can feel the history in every corner of the city. I really regard it as my second home. I have an unusual connection with the UK and I feel it is very special. China has had a long-standing special relationship with the UK."

"But you are still going to try to become a Canadian citizen?"

"Yes. It's practically impossible to be a British citizen if you are middle-class Chinese."

59

# SPRING

It just cannot be spring. But all the shops and public buildings have removed the tell-tale heavy cloth and felt flaps which normally shut out the biting cold from across the few doors that are not locked and barred against it. The apartment is freezing too and people are to be seen in their coats inside as the heating has been switched off and the sun has still to show its reluctant face through the pollution.

There are some signs of life around though. The trees and hedges of the parks and public space have been unwrapped from their winter coats of green fabric, secured with wooden batons and weighted ropes.

It is always rather endearing in early December to see the workers carefully wrapping up the city in its green coat of protective cloth. It is a very practical, if enormously expensive, exercise to wrap every public hedge and many of the bushes, shrubs and low trees across Beijing individually. I wonder if the greenery appreciates this touching care as it absorbs all that carbon belched out by the factories and transport system that otherwise choked Beijing for much of the year in a cough-inducing fug.

# Pollution and window cleaners

It catches the back of your throat. You wake up with a dry mouth and the feeling that someone has smeared your lips with coal. Welcome to Beijing in smog time. The rasping cough sounded like he'd been on 60 cigarettes-a-day all his life, but Mr Liang was contorted with the effort of clearing his throat, not due to the cheap cigarettes that until a recent change in the law used to stub out any vaguely healthy aspect of restaurants in China, but from living in Beijing.

Mr Liang runs a successful fruit shop just round the corner from where I live in the Chaoyang District of Beijing.

"Sounds like you have had a bad day Mr Liang?" I smile across the room and he shuffles over to my table and collapses in a disorderly heap into the chair opposite me.

"So you are not working today?" he counters in a gruff and growling manner that belies the smile on his face. He doesn't drink coffee but knows I'll pay so will have one of his endless teas.

"I'm a foreigner. We get days off!"

"You should have my job; never a day off."

"Bad cough Mr Liang."

I hit a nerve and he is off on his tirade, carefully focused on the failure of the local, rather than national, government to solve the crushingly atrocious smog and pollution in this enormous city, despite recent improvements. Received wisdom is that the pollution knocks up to 10 years off your life here and even small children are in hospital with respiratory problems.

A friend of mine told me recently that his wife had held their youngest back from kindergarten since the classroom air filter wasn't working. Some schools actually close when the official air quality index rises above 300. World Health Organization figures suggest that anything over 50 is hazardous. It's the noxious cocktail of carbon monoxide, sulphur dioxide and the particulates smaller than 2.5 microns that settle in your lungs and can't be eradicated. It's the grit in the air that you can actually taste when you land at the airport as the outside air is pumped in to greet you rather than scooped out of the atmosphere up at 10,000 metres.

You can tell when it is really bad because even the locals wear face masks. I must say, I was a little bemused once to see a local with a face mask on and a cigarette in his hand. "How does that work?" I remember thinking. "Which is the lesser of the two evils?

"Cigarettes," my colleague cynically remarked, "take the taste of the air away!"

Mr Liang directs his well-rehearsed and articulate attack at the singular failure, he opines, of the local authorities to stamp on, in no particular order: factory emissions from poorly run industry to the west and north west of the city, poor quality diesel used in the increased number of buses, too many cars on the streets, dust from construction of too many office blocks and shopping malls and, badly managed licence plate issuing which allows the rich to have two plates for the same car, to avoid the oft announced 'odd and even' number plate days.

This peculiar, but oft enacted, bylaw of Beijing means that if you have a car licence plate ending in an odd number, you could be banned from driving in to the city on alternate days of the week to those with an even number, if that makes sense! Bizarre as it seems, and broadly unenforceable in practice, this is supported by the local population who, by and large, abide by it. Not so the wealthy few, who simply do not bother with the nicety of a plate at all and if stopped haggle on the 'fee' payable to the policeman, or buy two, through whatever means they have available, and then use one or the other as appropriate by getting their driver to throw it randomly onto the back parcel shelf.

Mr Liang is still going strong and we seem to have been joined by both the coffeeshop owner and the man who I could have sworn was washing the windows a few minutes ago. All conclude that "something should be done", by "the authorities", and "the powers that be" need to "stop it right now". I could be back in my local pub in Yorkshire talking about traffic-calming measures on the main road through our village. It is the faceless bureaucrats of anywhere in the world at which the general public's venom is directed and here in Beijing, and many of the other severely polluted cities of modern China, it is no different.

## "Cigarettes," my colleague cynically remarked, "take the taste of the air away!"

The violent agreement subsides and my bill comes. I seem to have been charged for all of our drinks. Some things don't change wherever you are in the world!

# The lawyer

Oliver Zhang is a product of the new China. Born in Hangzhou and educated in China, in law, he spent two years in the UK at Nottingham, then Exeter, University in postgraduate studies, before returning to China to work. Now in his 30s, Oliver is a successful lawyer in Beijing, having spent 10 years in practice. But he has great ambitions to go further still.

During his time in the UK he fell in love.

"I fell in love across the political divide," he says wistfully. "My girlfriend was born in Taiwan from the Chiang Kai Check side of the politics. That meant we were always going to find life a struggle. I am from the mainland and she held a Republic of China passport. I remember when she had to go back to Taiwan and I saw her off on the aeroplane, I was speechless. We loved each other very much but we didn't know if we would ever see each other again because of the political differences between Taiwan and Mainland China".

Soon after she left, Oliver returned to his hometown of Hangzhou. They kept in touch.

"In those days (1990s) there was no international telephone link out of my home town so she used to phone me almost every day."

They resolved to overcome the difficulties and marry.

"Her father was against it. He had fought against the communists during the civil war. He felt she was marrying the enemy. I remember listening to that call from him. She was so embarrassed."

They married.

Oliver now has two young daughters living with his wife in Taiwan. He has spent months away from them and expects to continue to do so for at least another year. Furthering his career has meant some five years in Shanghai, and more recently, five more in Beijing, now in an international law firm. He speaks perfect English, with an English accent, rather than the mid-Atlantic one common in English-speaking Chinese, often educated in the US or by American/English teachers in China.

He worries about the education of his daughters and how to bring them up. "My wife and I talk about this all the time and I spend a little time each day considering my responsibilities. I think about how to support them in having an international perspective on China, proud to be both from Taiwan but also from the Mainland. It is a challenge, but I am determined that they will be able to benefit from the developments of China. They are part of the new generation of hope for the future, when we will all be just Chinese, not Taiwanese or Mainlanders."

There is another departure from the norm for Oliver and his wife. The young parents of today in China work, often away from home, like Oliver, or for long hours with long commuting into the cities where the work is. A daily slog of two hours in each direction is not uncommon in Beijing. As such, it is the grandparents of China who are bringing up the next generation. It is a situation Oliver and his wife do not feel is in the best interests of their children. His mother disagrees. "I need to help her though it is our decision," he muses. "It is difficult for her to accept and I know she feels a little lost and without purpose, but we really feel that the girls must be brought up by their mother and father. Not only will this mean that my wife and girls must come to the mainland to live as soon as possible, but also that my mother must come to terms with our desires for our children."

This decision on their children is a joint one between Oliver and his wife, another departure from the old ways of being male-dominated. "We speak every day and all our thinking is collaborative and joint."

"I miss them very much. But I know it will not be for ever and we will have a good life together."

Oliver pauses for a long time.

"At the end of the day I am a southerner and that is also a consideration." In this short phrase lies another of the Chinese complexities. In a country the size of Europe and more, it is inconceivable to most people that its diversity of geography can possibly be seen the same or treated the same. "It's like comparing the French with the English or the Italians with the Danes," says Oliver. Here, we all share the same basic language, though many different dialects, but that's about it. The differences between the provinces and specifically the northerners and the southerners, are immense in culture, ways of doing business, attitude, style of acting and so many other things."

Oliver expects to go back to Shanghai to further his career, and in an ideal world, to return to his hometown of Hangzhou.

"It's in my blood," he says. "I am proud to be from Hangzhou and I want the city to be successful and believe I can be part of, and contribute to, that success. At the end of the day, it is less than an hour on the high speed train from Shanghai which remains the international and commercial hub of China."

As Oliver is a lawyer, we discuss the changes in the profession in China. It is a very different system to elsewhere in the world and a complex web of evolving, as well as old, law. "There will be more change," speculates Oliver. "I see more and more Chinese firms of lawyers working to collaborate with international firms. There is incredible consolidation in the profession and mergers are regularly announced. As more and more Chinese business look overseas, and international business expands in China, there will be a great opportunity for business development. His firm is already expanding and work is being done in Kazakhstan and other states on the boarders of China as well as across the Association of South East Asian Nations (ASEAN) region.

The professions – law and accounting in particular – are relatively young, with many firms spawned from the government changes in the 1970s when hitherto government departments across the land were cut loose to compete in the market economy. Also, the old ways of work being given to friends, though the time-honoured notion of guangxi (personal relationships), is changing. It has by no means gone away, but the next generation of law, tax and accounting professionals are forging new relationships based on quality of work and market reputation, rather than relationships and introductions alone. "Clients are changing too," says Oliver. "They are looking at your credentials as a firm and as an individual, not just how well their boss knows your boss."

As this consummate professional discusses family, business and Beijing there is a distinct flavour of change in the manner and words he uses. There is a palpable enthusiasm and optimism as well as a willingness to embrace the differences and difficulties of China's turbulent past and to move on.

"I am excited about the future for China and I want my daughters to be part of it," he says. "I want to be part of it. Things move so fast here and there is so much opportunity. I know I need to be at the front of the charge, as those who are first will win long-term advantage. The West needs to understand that we are not going to wait around to get it 100% right first time. We will try and maybe fail, but failure itself will spur both myself and my country to greater things."

# A Woman of Substance

Yuan Rui Ming is an elegant and poised woman. Born in 1952, she wears her years gracefully but in her eyes as she talks you can see the pain of the history which makes her the woman she is today. Mother of Oliver Zhang, (interviewed in chapter 9) she speaks no English, so her son acts as a patient and respectful translator.

"My grandfather was from Jia Shan, a small town in Zhe Jiang province," she begins. "He was an accountant. My grandmother was from another small town, Shao Xing, not far away, a housewife. She brought up my father and ....." She pauses. "Is this what you want to hear?"

"Of course," I reply. Her eyes search mine for clues. She does not want to bore me or say too much perhaps?

"Where did you grow up?" I ask.

"Hangzhou. In those days, it was a small historical city, quiet, not like today. Now it is an international tourist city. The railway station at that time was shabby. We lived close to the railway tracks then. Now, Hangzhou East railway station is the biggest railway station in Asia. The house we lived in was demolished to make way for the West Lake Avenue. There has been such significant change. I never dreamed about that level of change. It has been so fast."

Like many of her generation, Rui Ming has experienced more and seen more change than any generation ever before. Her story is that of the rise to economic supremacy of China.

"You have to be proud of China, to make these changes in just 30 years. It never happened in the West." There is no pride in her quiet voice, only facts.

Rui Ming was at school in Hangzhou; she tells me that the elementary school is still there. She graduated from elementary school after six years and entered high school. Just six months later, the Cultural Revolution started.

"It was 1966. School stopped. I was only 14 years old. I was supposed to graduate in 1968 but I couldn't. We were forced to stop. We all had to go to the rural areas to help the peasants to do farming. It was called 'chadvi'. We had to go."

The words are flat and precise, clear and unemotional. She was sent to a small countryside village called Jianshan. She remembers it very clearly.

"Only a few neighbours of a similar age went to the same area with me, but not to the same village. I was on my own. After schooling stopped, all the students were brought together at a local resident committee. We were registered and the committee sent us, allocated us, to different places. It was quite fast. I can remember thinking. "Wow! What just happened here?" I felt it was a total waste of four years. I cried a lot. I lost my golden years as a girl."

Her eyes never leave mine as she speaks. As I make my notes she pauses and picks up the story with my eyes. Her gaze is kind and thoughtful. She wants to tell her story. Although one of millions who went through this time, for her it was once. It was her life. She wants me to hear it, understand it, from her, first hand. Despite the clear pain of the memories of the time, Rui Ming is purposeful and dignified in the recounting of her story.

"Even the peasants questioned why we were there, why the government had done this. I dressed like a peasant, I ate, I slept, I worked like a peasant. I became a peasant. When the holiday came, the national holiday of Chinese New Year, I remember I was sent to cut down trees in the mountains. I was in tears. On this special day, this important day for family, I was on some unknown mountain hundreds of kilometres from the people I loved. I was very home-sick."

She smiles at me. The warmth is palpable. There is no anger or resentment in her voice or her words. Just acceptance of a time now long past but with strong memories.

"There were no phones then. We could only write letters. In the beginning I would be able to write about every 20 days. Later, I got used to it and would write about one letter a month. After four years, there was a change in government policy. If you only had one child, then that child was allowed to return to work in a factory in Hangzhou, so they could take care of their parents. So I was allowed to go back."

"There were some changes in Hangzhou but not many in the four years I had been away. I was sent to make clothes in a local garment factory. It was only 25 minutes' walk from our house. Although I had to work eight hours-a-day, compared to the countryside it was paradise. Also, I learned the skill of making clothes."

She is talking more brightly now, her features becoming more animated as she remembers this time, clearly significantly better than before. It was at the factory that she met her husband.

"I was 24 years old. He was the brother of my grandfather's neighbour. He was one of 10 children. He was number seven I remember. There were 12 children but two died in infancy. It was unusual to only have one child in those days. I was one of five children but two died in the womb and my two brothers died very early, after only 30 and 40 days. I was the only one left."

The facts fall like rain. It is difficult to take it in at the speed of delivery. The reality of the situation, starkly and simply told. This is a story recounted across millions of Chinese from this generation. It is possible to read of all this in the detached pages of history and to see the pictures in the museums or watch the faded propaganda films of the time. But here it was in front of me, inescapable, personal, poignant and true.

"Are you ok?" she asks. "Should I carry on?"

I am suddenly aware that I have stopped listening. My own mind is full of images conjured up from her descriptions. I apologize and explain that her story is really making me think. She smiles again and seems pleased.

"I spent 15 years in the factory in different departments," she continues. "First, I was on the production line and then in the accounting department. I became an accountant. So I moved from peasant, to worker, to management. I got to use my brain. I liked the work and the pressure."

That smile again.

"We were married in 1978 and our only son was born later that same year. My husband was a driver. It was a good job in those days. Good jobs were doctors, soldiers, drivers. He was from Shao Xing. He worked for the Electricity Bureau, part of the government, which later became State Grid after 2001."

I am curious. These were times of significant change in China, was she aware of the changes going on?

"Oh yes, very aware. Everyone around me watched the news on the TV. We were aware that there was enormous change going on. In general, we felt it was positive. Specifically, salaries were going up so we felt the benefits directly. We had to use ration coupons in the early days to get most things such as food and basics. After the revolution, the coupons disappeared so it was clear change, positive change, was happening".

In meeting people around China and talking about the days of the 1980s, the same story emerges from everyone to whom I speak, and Rui Ming is no different. There had been immense suffering and displacement of people, true. State enterprise factories required long hours and hard work, true. There were many changes, many difficulties and many problems, true. But for the workers in the factories and for those such as Rui Ming, with her new husband and newly born son, things were improving dramatically on the ground and in their everyday lives. There may have been propaganda, but the reality of better quality, and more, food, rising wages, eradication of ration coupons and the like serve to remind me to try to retain a broader perspective on history. Listening to those such as Rui Ming provides a different view as to what it was like at the grass roots in society.

"For young people, society became far more open," explains Rui Ming. "The earlier government restrictions were lifted. Department stores had had very limited choice, but slowly we noticed more and more products appearing on the shelves. There was more choice available too of different variants of products for customers. I personally noticed changes in the book stores. First, all the books and pamphlets were on political subjects only, but then I started to see more and more books on culture, history, and novels."

In the following 10 years, Rui Ming and her husband continued to work in the same businesses, and by the early 1990s, things had taken a further 'leap forward'.

"Compared with the previous 10 years there were even more material changes and you could actually feel the economy growing really fast. Importantly, attitudes were changing fast too. We became more and more aware of globalization and that China was part of a much wider world. We were looking for communications from, and with, the rest of the world. There was a real hunger for it. People were willing to exchange views and opinions. Before then, people were very closed. In the early 1990s, everything changed and people were really far more open minded."

There is genuine animation and excitement in Rui Ming's voice as she recounts these years. Married, and her son growing up, life was better for her, her family and her peers than it had ever been before. The days of being a peasant were almost a forgotten memory.

"With our son growing up, my husband and I felt the pressure to earn more money to raise him. We also realized the importance of education. An education we had both lost to history. We studied hard in our spare time. Partly, it was so we could keep pace with our son's education, but also so we could improve ourselves and our own jobs. I learned to become an accountant and my husband studied economics and management."

The energy of her descriptions and words affect me powerfully. It is clear that this young married couple, a product of the revolution, were grasping every shred of opportunity which came their way, and creating more almost out of thin air, through sheer hard work and application. An eight-hour day in the factory preceded by an early morning start and a late finish probably didn't leave much time to spend with their son, let alone study an alien subject.

"The driver jobs were disappearing, but because my husband was a good driver he was promoted to the Head of the Drivers Department at the company. It was his responsibility to arrange all the drivers' schedules and arrangements. Then he was promoted again to the Public Safety Department, in charge of safety in the whole business. He became a superintendent. A very good job. A good job meant that he had to study hard to do it well."

Now she is beaming with pride at me. Undoubtedly, they had now moved from very difficult times to a much better situation. Her husband was clearly a success and through hard work and application money was more plentiful.

"At that time, we were three generations living together in one house. But with my husband's promotion, we were able to move to a bigger house, though still in Hangzhou."

The pride is palpable. But this story was not boastful, just the truth, proudly told, of achievement, almost against the odds, from an inauspicious start. The next 20 years from the 1990s to today also told a story of change. Both she and her husband retired in 2002 and 2003 respectively. Their son married and had two girls. Now Rui Ming is a grandmother, still living in Hangzhou but visiting her son in Beijing. His family is in Taiwan and she is here to spend precious time with him.

"Now I have no real worry about the rest of my life," she says. "I am retired, I am a grandmother and my son is a successful lawyer. I am so very proud of my son and his achievements. I have seen him grow through difficult times to be a student and now a father. I hope he will have a prosperous future and achieve much better things than we did."

"And what of China now?" I ask.

"I am very optimistic about China compared to the past 30 years. Particularly after President Xi has taken power there has been, and I am sure will be, another series of changes in China. This recent wave of change has reassured me about my optimism for this country. As it becomes more prosperous then the people can enjoy that prosperity."

These are not the words from a recent propaganda pamphlet or the TV news. This articulate, self-schooled and self-improved woman has experienced the recent and most turbulent history of China, from the Cultural Revolution, through the Great Leap Forward to the emergence as a world superpower and influencer of the global economy. She has recounted how it has felt on the ground. Her words are her own, personal and unabridged perspective, over a cup of coffee in the heart of Beijing. No one is around to listen, other than her son, beaming with pride for his mother.

So what hopes does Yuan Rui have for her grandchildren?
"I hope that my granddaughters will have the opportunity to see the world

and travel. To become aware of the world and to increase their understanding of it. There is still not a great enough interaction between the ordinary people of China and the rest of the world. The more there is in the next generations, then the better it will be for China and for us all.

"I am so optimistic for the future of China and the next generation. The main reason for this is that people of my age really had to struggle to manage and survive. It is very different now with a much more stable life. This is a better place to start.

"We are lucky. Money is not as important to me as before. My health, and the health of my family, is the most important thing now."

Rui Ming's final comment is a reminder of the reality of the current China. Economic prosperity has brought improvements to all in the country.

However, there is a cost.

# The professor

Paul Gillis PhD is a leading scholar of the accounting profession in China, based at the Guanghua School of Management at the famous Peking University in Beijing. Despite many years working internationally, latterly in China, he has neither lost his distinctive American accent, nor his well-developed scepticism of all things smelling of self-promotion or pomposity. After more than four decades first in, then observing, the accounting industry, he has seen cataclysmic change both globally and specifically in China, where the profession itself is really only 15 or so years old. He has an acute sense of humour and the honed cynicism of someone who has heard every excuse in the book, and a few more besides, from students and business people alike.

"I wanted an international career," he says, rocking back in his chair, which he fills with his considerable frame, developed through his American college football days. "My 28 years in a big international accounting firm working in Singapore, the US and China, as well as numerous other countries, certainly gave me that!" When he laughs his whole frame laughs with him. He has an urbane and warm smile, which seems to wrap his whole body. Paul is an intensely likeable man.

He has neither the (perhaps) expected shambling gait of the crusty professor or the clipped arrogance of the incredibly intelligent academic. His personality fills the room with benign benevolence and sharp wit.

"I took early retirement from accounting to do my PhD and then stayed on as a professor here at Guanghua to teach." I learned later that he chose to leave when the politics and in-fighting took up more of his time than his beloved tax work. He is a principled man. "I've been fortunate to be able to work closely with the global regulators, specifically the American ones, as well as with leaders here in China for many years. That's given me a really interesting perspective which people seem to want to hear about." He is a regular commentator on the accounting profession and accounting standards, both globally and their application, or likely application, in China. Paul is the author of a seminal book on the, some would say, arcane subject of 'The Big Four and the development of the accounting profession in China'. He also has a well-followed blog and is oft quoted in the Western press on accounting matters in relation to China.

"I'm not always popular with the profession or some of the firms' leadership for what I say but I believe it needs to be said. There is a need to expose the illogical and ill-conceived responses and approaches that some people seem to think are acceptable in a world where standards and regulations are pushing for more and more transparency and better and better governance."

Does he ever get told off by the business school or even worse, by government bodies, for his remarks?

"I have a passion for both the accounting profession, which I study and focus on, and business education in China, which I practise and earn my living from. People know I am speaking from the heart and with significant, deep and experienced knowledge of the subject. Yes, I do get complaints, usually from the big accounting firm leadership, but the Dean of the School here is a supporter and encourages me to speak out on the things that matter. In my mind, if I get no complaints, then I am probably not doing my job!"

"So what of the developments in business education in China? Isn't it rather underdeveloped?" I ask.

"Business education in China started 30 years ago. The Guanghua School is 30 years old this year (2015). It has a long and distinguished history. In reality, the school has been at the forefront of Chinese business education. In the early days, the Chinese imported mainly Western PhDs. Many were US, but ethnically Chinese, returners. There was a hunger for, and adoption of, Western MBA-style education techniques. These people had expertise in business, economics and the Western approach, but none of the Chinese relevance or experience in Chinese business or even a Chinese education. Those days 15 to 20 years ago were raw. So, really, Chinese business education then was not very Chinese.

"Of course, the lessons on GE, Ford, global conglomerates and the successes of Western entrepreneurs were interesting to the Chinese students of the day from an academic perspective, but they couldn't apply the lessons locally. China was changing then, but it was not changed, we needed to be more relevant."

The past ten years, Paul tells me, have been characterized by the faculty generating much more research and knowledge about doing business in China and the 'Chinese Way'.

"We now teach much more about doing business in China from a Chinese perspective," he attests. "There are unique challenges and issues in Chinese business and we focus on these. Everyone wants to know about Jack Ma and the rise of Alibaba but there are other stories to be told about the way successful Chinese businesses grow and succeed."

We warm to our common subject of doing business in China. Management structure, leadership, governance and decision making are all examined. I am reminded that all business schools remain under state control, as education is, by and large, the world over. While this doesn't seem to affect the quality or rigour of the research, it brings with it a degree of inflexibility. However, this too is changing. Paul agrees that the business schools will have to focus more on getting closer to business.

"In the West, the Dean and the members of the senate or school leadership are out in the business community raising finance. In China, they are inside the party infrastructure so academia and business is not as fully integrated as they are in the West. But it is changing and will change further. It has to do so as student demands for education more relevant to the real world is increasing."

So what are the new insights coming from the increased research into the success stories of Chinese entrepreneurs and business?

"There has not been much developed about the Chinese business approach as yet - many businesses themselves are young and a product of the extraordinary growth of the wider Chinese economy. However, there are trends and specific issues emerging. One area of study is around how Chinese business leaders have learned the ability to manage large-scale operations. Some of the state-owned, and a significant number of non-state, businesses have multiple millions of employees. The scale is unimaginable in the West. The skill required to keep such enterprises running is significant, all the more so to keep them profitable and growing."

What will happen now that the growth in China is slowing down? Will the skills to manage the upsurge be matched by those needed when growth evaporates. Also, how do businesses of the size and scale of those seen in China manage without diaries? This seeming reluctance of Chinese business, and indeed the Chinese people, to engage in any form of planning has been a source of long-standing curiosity to me personally, and is often at the root of many Western business failures in China. The difference in planning and executing in the West and in China is a seemingly unbridgeable chasm in the eyes of many Western business people I meet.

"For sure it's a difference and there is a genuine reluctance of Chinese leaders to engage in planning," says Paul. "On the positive side, it means there is immense flexibility and agility in business. However, it also means there is a reticence for leaders and corporations to commit to even medium-term objectives, for fear that it might restrict their flexibility to take advantage of new opportunities. Broadly, I think the jury is out on this. It is a very Chinese thing and a reason so many Western business people get so unbelievably frustrated when working here. The Chinese will never commit to a meeting more than a week in advance, in case they have to offend you by saying they have to go somewhere else; that, basically, they have someone more important to see than you. In the West, we all understand that meetings change and so do priorities. Also, senior people's diaries are planned up to a year in advance, at least in principle. However, here in China with the concept of 'face', they just can't bring themselves to succumb to it."

I was reminded that this happens all the time in China and on the grandest of scales. It was only late in the day on 24 December 2014 that the government released the holiday calendar for 2015, including the fact that 2 January 2015 was going to be a holiday, and that everyone in China would be expected to work on 4 January to 'make up' for the day of holiday.

This approach to holidays is another probably little-understood, or widely-known, story. It is well-accepted in China, and by the Chinese population, that holidays are optional. You don't get paid for them and you only get the national holidays and the government decides when they are. Of course, individual business can add holiday terms to their working practices as they see fit. But the only guarantees are the national holidays. In addition, there is a general practice that if you get a day off, then you work a day the next weekend to make up the time. Time off for extra personal holidays can be taken, at the discretion of management, but you don't get paid for it, unless you either work for a foreign-owned company or are very, very lucky to work for one of the new wave of enlightened Chinese entrepreneurs. I heard a story of an interview with a Chinese business leader who, when asked why he expected his staff to work seven-days-a-week, replied, "well, what would they do with the time off?" It may be apocryphal, but it has too much of a ring of familiarity to me.

"Board meetings are not planned". Paul is on the topic of governance. "You could argue that they don't have time for preparing the papers for the meetings as things change so fast here that the agenda is out of date immediately it is published, perhaps two weeks in advance. Of course, there are exceptions, but they are few and far between."

So does this lack of forward planning in business affect the competitiveness of China? The government issues regular 'directional' five-year plans and has done for years.

"[It's] hard to say, as we haven't really got the long-term horizons of business here to make a real judgement. However, a lack of strategic planning might reduce competitiveness in the short term, but my belief is that the agility and flexibility they gain is highly competitive. Where Western business can be atrophied by the paralysis of analysis and over-planning, Chinese businesses can turn on a dime and move to take advantage of economic or market changes. I guess the ideal is somewhere in-between. However, there is much to learn from Chinese businesses in the way they adapt to new developments and opportunities. Fortunes have been made because of the agility of decision making they exhibit."

How does the accounting profession cope in this environment?

"The Chinese accounting profession is changing and our teaching is based on the technical and societal aspects of accounting, just as anywhere else in the world. There is a disconnect between the needs of the profession and the needs of business. Public accounting in China is less high profile than it used to be. It used to be seen as prestigious, and in the 1990s, many international firms got licences. The supply of graduates was way lower than the needs of the profession. The big international firms mainly recruited people who could speak English and then trained them up. Now it has changed and there is a widespread view that the profession is a tough place to work. Even the domestic firms are having problems recruiting bright young graduates to work for them. The state-owned enterprises and government departments are seen as better opportunities as are the larger privately-held, stock-based, businesses and investment banks. Consequently, students are drawn there and not to the profession. It is true around the world, not just in China. The professional services career path is seen as a long and a difficult one."

Our discussion turns to the students themselves. Getting into university in China is notoriously difficult, even more so the top ones. Both Paul and I agree that this bodes well for the running of businesses in China in the future. Bright, well-educated, internationally-minded, and often experienced, students, are moving into the corporate, government and professional worlds alike.

"This is good for the future of business in China and for China itself," says Paul. "Although there is a difference between the foreign approach to corporate governance and that of the West. The basic concept of the foreign approach to governance is that separation of roles at the top of an organization enables mitigation against fraud and poor behaviour. Collusion is theoretically easier in China due to the strict 'laws' of hierarchy, relationships (guangxi) and 'face' (面子 mian zi). This means that practices that commonly mitigate against fraud in the West cannot be relied upon in China. This is where the anti-graft focus introduced by the Chinese political leadership in the past two years has worked and is working. There seems to be a greater awareness that there are now real consequences to poor behaviour, corruption and profiteering. You have to hope it will continue to shake people into changing behaviours that, if you read Chinese history, have been around for hundreds of years."

I do read it, and corruption has been endemic in China throughout the 5,000 years of its history, not just hundreds. It will need a significant and consistent effort over a long period of time to shake the habits of generations. Having well-trained, highly intelligent, internationally savvy graduates will boost the gene pool of good governance, to the wider benefit of business as a whole.

Considering the position on anti-graft Paul's view is that the widespread, and widely publicized, focus on the misdemeanours of a number of high profile foreign owned multinationals and joint owned ventures in the past few years was understandable, even desirable.

"Many of the managers of these businesses didn't understand the rules here in China. They unwittingly stepped over the line. Having said that, there were many who did things that they would never do in their own countries. It is probably easier to focus on foreign-owned businesses than to do so on domestically-owned ones where political connections add complexity. But the message is clear to everyone. Chinese businesses are next in line for scrutiny and sanction".

Perhaps the Chinese saying, "you have to kill a chicken to scare the monkey" applies here.

After so many years in China observing the accounting professionals and being at the heart of the emerging business education sector, what lessons does Paul have for Western businesses?

He pauses for a while as he considered the question. He is an American through and through, one who takes the Christmas, Western New Year and Chinese New Year holidays in Northern California to escape the chilled winds and heavy pollution of Beijing in January. However, he has learned to be Chinese too, he has a Chinese wife and a job that is at the heart of Chinese academia.

"First, I have certainly learned that Chinese and Westerners are much more alike than they are different. Chinese business people are just like you and me. All too often, foreigners here see things as dramatically different and they lose their basic ideals and values. The lesson is to be authentic, be yourself. Authenticity is genuine and true. It will get you further and it will get you more respected."

Again a long pause, long for Paul anyway, he adds:

"Second, I believe that China's best years are ahead of her. I'm bullish for China. As living standards rise towards those of the West, the world does not have the natural and other resources to feed and sustain another 1.3 billion 'Americans'. I feel the answer is neither to hold back China nor to reduce the US lifestyle. It needs to be looked at in the round."

# Being gay in China

Harry (Zhu Wan Yu) is waiting for me outside the coffeeshop. It is not even open yet. We are early but I am expecting her. Short cut hair, casual androgynous clothing and boyish features speak of individualism and a strong sense of self.

Born in 1988, 'Harry' is one of the growing number of Chinese who have come out and openly acknowledge that they are gay.

"I left home after middle school and went to Canada at the age of 16. I was 24 when I came back. I was at high school in Vancouver in Canada, then attended York University in Toronto and read economics. Eight years is a long time in China, so when I came back, there were really no friends here who could help me build my career so I have had to build it up from zero."

Harry is open, engaging and direct. She makes no effort to hide who she is or how she feels. This is in stark contrast to the otherwise broadly closed community of gay people in China. Though they are increasingly more vocal in both Shanghai and Beijing, there is little to tell of their community outside these two more international and cosmopolitan of cities.

"My father has always pushed me to do something but has never told me exactly, "do this" or "do that". He just asked me to think of what I wanted for myself. I really appreciate that from him. He is still in Tianjin, where he is a self-made man, an entrepreneur. He has a business making sensors for the electronics industry. He worked at a German electronics company for 10 years and then set up on his own and has been very successful. I came to Beijing from Tianjin in 2012 as it was too difficult for me there. It was too small and too slow a pace for me."

I felt that maybe staying in her home town would also mean Harry would be recognized as different and it would have been continually difficult for her parents to have her there as an unmarried, and so visibly independent and different, daughter. My feeling is that the loss of face in the local community for her parents may well have contributed to the feeling of claustrophobia and 'cabin fever' which pushed the move to Beijing.

Her look is piercing at times. She has a quiet confidence and self-assurance born of knowing who she is, what she believes in and what she wants from life. She sips coffee between pouring out her words. But there is a pace and clarity to her delivery which draws you into her story and touches you to the core. She is quiet and shy in many ways, but determined to speak out about who she is and what she stands for.

"I went to an international school in Dalian until grade 10 and they had a strong Canadian connection with Sentinel school in Western Vancouver. So I managed to go there for two years, staying with a Taiwanese family who had a house there. It's supposed to be the nicest community in Canada and I really enjoyed it. I came back home for two months in the summer each year but chose to stay over and attend summer school for two months each year too."

"I lived on my own for four years when I did a Masters at York University in Toronto. I rented an apartment not far from the campus. My father helped me. I was not very outgoing and a little shy so most of the time I kept myself to myself and stayed in more often than I went out. I learned karate in my spare time and didn't have many friends. Actually, I was quite fat in Canada! Too much good food. When I came back home and my mother came to collect me from the airport she didn't recognize me as I looked so different! I was fat and had yellow hair too. The second time she didn't recognize me either as I had lost the weight and changed my hair again."

Her individuality was clear both to her and to her family from her teenage years at middle school. Her father supported her from the very start, though her mother has taken a while to accept her difference; maybe, I feel, she still hasn't.

"I came back to China for my family. They never thought about emigration and I was very lonely in Canada so I came home. I didn't feel that economics as a degree would help me develop a career as I really didn't see myself in a bank - I knew I wouldn't fit in. I really wanted and want to be different."

"How?"

"Everything really, I look different with my very short hair and I never wear a skirt. I have my own ideas and I don't do what people tell me I should do. I don't agree with the pressure from society here, to conform to the expected norm. Most women of my age are supposed to be married. I don't accept it."

She speaks calmly, but there is strength and more than a hint of defiance in the words and tone. Here is a young woman who is strongly individual and has the underlying strength of character to carry it through in the most difficult of circumstances and against the strongest of societal norms.

"My parents accept that I am different. My father just wants me to be happy every day. Most Chinese parents say they want their children to be happy, but in reality they can't do it as 'being happy' means to conform to the society norms. The pressure is really high but I would say that while Chinese society cares that I am gay and sees it as outside normality, 80% of people you meet really don't care. They are just getting on with their own lives. I'd say 90% of Chinese parents care deeply about the sexuality of their children. However, when I told my father, he was not surprised and he encouraged me to be happy. He said it is not important. I am not hurting anyone and no one is affected other than me. I realized I was gay when I was a teenager. It was just clear to me and I accepted it."

So now you are in Beijing, are you working?

"Yes, I am in the film industry. It is quite a new business. Owned by a friend of my father. I worked in the Beijing Bookworm Bookstore (a famous location in Beijing as a library, bookstore, coffeeshop and bar) for the first three months I was here. One day, I took a phone call from my father and he asked me ... "Do you want to go into the film business?" I said "yes" and met the guy my father knew. He had expected me to be a big fan of movies, but I wasn't! He was a bit surprised but he wanted to give me a chance, so he sent me to work for a media company he knew in Beijing. They were creating a database of films and I helped to set it up. I was there for a year".

Here lies the story of many people of Harry's generation. Jobs come from connections and connections come from deep-rooted friendships of family more often than not. Helping the daughter or son of a friend cements the bonds of relationships so important in China. Guangxi (relationships) are what China has run on for thousands of years and it isn't changing any time soon. It's as much about who you know, or who your family know, as it is about qualifications, intelligence and application. Harry's story is a common one as the next generation of China's educated middle classes expands and develops. It is repeated across China's society, but among the emerging and burgeoning middle classes, it is particularly strong as a boost to start people off on their careers.

"I stopped that job after a year as I wanted to study again. However, my father's friend said he didn't want me to go back to school but to get more experience. I agreed to work for him and study in my own time. Self-study is hard, I have to learn on my own and I do find this really tough. I read a lot of books so I can learn about the film industry and film-making. I have also been reading and learning a lot about Chinese history. I lost all that learning about the history of my own country by going to Canada. I never thought about it as a teenager. However, now I think it is really important. If you can understand your own country's history then you can understand your culture better. I have read a lot about the culture of my country. History is made up of people, and people make history. This is really important to me now."

To lose a grip on history in China is almost to lose your identity. People tell me that you are not truly Chinese unless you understand the subtleties of the culture, and the culture is driven not just by the language, complex as that is, but by the detailed and ingrained history taught through all schools and across all ages. There is just so much to absorb that coming to it late in life, and on your own, is almost too much. Harry seems to be struggling with this element of her own identity, without which she will always be even more of the outsider she has already chosen to be. I know this from a personal perspective, that despite my lack of language skills, just understanding some of China's deep and complex history has already unlocked an understanding which I would never have had if I just tried to absorb it as I worked and lived here. Even as I barely scratch the surface, I learn more and more and expand my understanding. But I am not Chinese. The power of the draw and the hunger to understand is almost irresistible if you are.

"The film industry in China is very different to that in the rest of the world," continues Harry. "In Chinese films, there is almost no planning. If you are the director, you also have to do everything else, script, lighting, everything. It is a hard job to master everything. The normal rules in the West for film are not applied in China. We have learned much from Hollywood and from the West but the industry here wants to make films that are run to our own, Chinese, rules. Also, the government has a perspective on all films and there are really strong guidelines. We can't tell ghost stories, the bad guy cannot prevail and you can't talk about gay people. We are constrained a good deal, but we have to accept it and things continue to change."

This perspective on film and the industry is also commented on elsewhere in these Notes (Chapter 17), specifically by Professor Huang, Dean of The Beijing Film Academy. Harry is candid about the influence of censorship on film and its production. Widely known and understood, the Chinese censorship department for the film industry has the right to demand changes to script and style right up to the last minute of release. In the words of a friend, "it is what it is" and people just have to accept it as part of the growing pains of this fast-growth economy. Indeed, there are recent examples of films being released and then cut or amended post release. There are strict rules on what you can show, including how much bare flesh in a shot. Low-cut dresses which reveal too much are not deemed appropriate and much debate prevails on the internet of post-production amendments to some quite high-profile films which first passed the reviews only to be subsequently amended three or four days after general release. The industry rolls with these punches and remains highly competitive and is growing at breakneck speed.

So what will the future hold for Harry?

"I am enjoying doing interesting things. I am really interested in what I am doing and every day at work is different. It suits me and who I am."

What will she be doing in five years' time?

"I hope my name will be in the credits of a movie. Maybe I will have written a script, which has become a film. I want to make a story about real life, gay life, but I don't know if even in five years' time it would be allowed to be published or released. I want to make a movie about our generation. Many people of my age don't really think about things deeply. They just adhere to the norm, the expectations that society seems to have of them, that parents have of them, that friends and neighbours have of them."

Harry is a very determined and resolute character. Her words are deliberate, thoughtful and heartfelt. She is reticent at times, but there is no lack of self-assurance or confidence in her ideas and views. She wears her sexuality easily and as a matter of fact. There is none of the ambiguity of position so often found in other gay Chinese people who seem to feel the need to conform, even to marry, for the sake of family 'face'. There is not even the slightest hint of that in Harry.

"I want to tell the story of the modern Chinese woman, those who have the inner strength to be different. This will be a new language for the people of China and for my generation. When you learn a language, it is not just the words and the grammar you need to know, but the history and the culture as well, to really understand. I believe that my story and the story of people like me also needs to be told in China. We are part of the new culture of the country and as such need to speak out and be heard as equals, contributing equally to making our country successful, as distinctly and proudly Chinese."

I rather think the story will be told more and more, and strongly sense that Harry will be one of the proud participants and active narrators.

# Youth culture

Mathew (Shao) Ma describes himself as a rich kid who "lost everything" and who now has "nothing to lose". He has the clothes and demeanour of a man on a mission to make a success of himself in the film industry. He certainly looks the part, of which he is proud. A small, mousey girl who he never introduces, but who seems like a cross between adoring fan, girlfriend and executive assistant, accompanies him. She says almost nothing for three hours.

Born in Shandong in 1993, one of five children, he tells me with a wry smile that his parents had to have three girls before they got the boy they wanted. Him. Then had another boy just to make sure. He was born into a rich family who had created significant wealth from building real estate, then, when Mathew was 16, his father lost everything.

"We had everything and then lost it all. I don't know what happened. Suddenly we had no money. What could I do? I decided to drop out of school and go and earn money to help my family. I went into the building trade. I just worked as hard as I could and earned about ¥1.0m by the time I was 17 years old!"

He is beaming from ear-to-ear with an impish grin that is impossible not to return. The phone rings and he passes it to his 'Girl Friday'. She wanders off to deal with it.

"I wanted more. I didn't think there was much more building work to be done in my home town, it had already been done. Well, I may have been wrong about that but I wanted to get into the service industry, less hard work manually and more using my brain. I decided to open my own restaurant and I had this idea that we could do something no one else had done, have a Chinese fast food place that was like McDonalds but for Chinese food. We set up in Shenzhen. I had to learn how to create a business and, along with three other shareholders, all of whom were older than me, we had a go at it. Now I know that location is everything in retail, use of colour and design too. Unfortunately, we got it wrong and after six months it was still not making any money. I was 18 years old."

"Hao is coming." 'Girl Friday' reports back.

It seems the call earlier was from Hao.

Mathew's parents told him to go back to college. So he did. But not just any college to learn an academic subject such as history, economics or business; he chose to become an actor.

"I am always questioning authority and teachers. It made me unpopular at school and at college but I decided to learn acting and spent a year as a model."

He rummages through his pockets and extracts a well-used wallet from which he draws a faded photograph of a muscular and tanned bodybuilder model. Himself at the age of 18.

"I've not got that body now," he muses

He looks ruefully at the photograph before folding it carefully back into his wallet and secreting it away into his voluminous coat.

"Also, I found out that the restaurant business had grown to having more than 40 sites and was making a lot of money. I had a 30% share of that when I left. It would have been worth a fortune but now I had nothing."

The phone rings again and the unassuming mousey girl takes it away.

"I went to the Chinese Central Academy of Arts to learn acting."

This is probably one of the most famous acting schools in China, though how he got in seems a little sketchy.

"People thought I was crazy. I wanted to be at the top of the film industry. I thought I wanted to be a director, so I spent the next six months learning everything I could about being a director. That's when I met Hao."

Hao is coming he again informs me, via his 'Girl Friday'.

"I produced my first film with Hao. We were at school together, it was ok, but not that great, but a good start."

He pulls out his laptop and sets about powering it up and searching for the film. He keeps talking at the same time. Words and self-expression are certainly not out of reach for this ambitious and talented young man. The film is actually rather good, short and shot with many different angles and clever camera work. Not that I know much about film, but the young actor at its heart seems pretty good to me. There is little too much metaphor for my liking overall, but then I am a bit of a philistine when it comes to cult and new style film.

"I decided I wanted to start a film company. You need a lot of government stuff to start a company."

I took it he meant paperwork and licences. The phone again. Hao, I guessed, was being challenged with navigation.

"It was hard work to get everyone convinced that I could do it but I managed to sort it out and was the youngest guy ever to set up a film company in China. I realized that I needed to be an owner of a film company, that it was best to own it rather than be an employee. Now six months later, I know how to make films. I started and had 40 workers, then three months later I had spent all the money, it's all gone now so it's just Hao and me. But we never gave up. We've just signed the papers for a deal worth ¥2m (£218.9k). Not much, but it's a start I guess."

He pauses from the delivery of his verbal onslaught.

"You know, there is only one way for the poor to become rich in China. Go to the cities. That's the only thing to do. That's what we did. We want to produce more films, that's what we want to do."

The phone rings yet again. It's Hao.

"We will succeed, you know. Most people don't know how to run a company. They don't have the vision of the future. I'm 21 years old and I want to launch an initial public offering (IPO) in five years' time."

The prospect of Mathew at the helm of a listed corporation intrigues me, to say the least, but I remain silent for now.

"In 2015, I'm going to set up three companies, an agency, a publishing business and a film company, so I can do everything from top to bottom and control it all personally. How can I do that?"

The question had wandered across my mind I must admit, though it was dragging its feet, as he delivered his waterfall of insight and ambition.

"I'll tell you. The market is more open now than it has ever been before. The opportunity for new films is enormous. We can't produce Western-style films due to our culture. People don't question the new style of new films; there is a new way of making films. Chinese filmmakers will get more down to earth, more Chinese. There are a lot of Chinese film producers with great opportunities for new styles of films all the time."

He reels off a string of names, some of which I recognize, but most are a blur of Chinese, as unfamiliar as the language.

"I want to develop a TV show, I am working on it now. We have a real chance."

"Where is the money coming from?" I ask

"What?"

"The money - where is it coming from, who are the investors, TV shows are expensive aren't they?"

"Oh, yeah, the money. To get the money - I'll let you into a secret. To my workers, I say, I have the money. To the investors, I say, I have the workers. It's simple."

"Really?" I can't help but be a little bit sceptical, but this is China and strange things happen to young entrepreneurs with attitude and good ideas.

"I am unusual..."

Hao arrives mid-sentence bringing with him man hugs and high fives.

Hao is a reserved and thoughtful, somewhat introspective 22 year old who has the honour of having two of China's most famous singers as his parents. We acquire a tea and a stool for him. He hunches into his designer white collarless shirt and expensive jacket and listens in.

"I'm unusual..."

We restart where Mathew left off

"I am not afraid to try anything. Many people are afraid to fail. I am not afraid to fail. We have nothing to lose. It's so easy. When I have fear then I just confront it."

He bangs the table and grabs the air with theatre that would fit well in a Shakespearean masterpiece. He has learned his craft well.

"In a year's time, my future is about life. I need to watch my health. In 10 years' time I will be more successful. I want to still have problems to solve though. I want to have my companies, I want to learn fast and get known by the top people, use the friendships, use the good people around me."

"Attitude is essential and having future thinking. These are the attributes of good and successful people. Only I see my future. My day is listening to music, writing and thinking. I am thinking all the time. I have two projects right now, the TV programme, and another one. And the money comes in."

"Remind me about that part?" I asked again.

"Look. To get money you just need three things. First, you have to look the part, you need to look rich. Good clothes, good looks. Second, you have to look friendly. If you don't look friendly who is going to believe that you will do anything? And third, you have to look like you are hopeful and thinking about the future."

"So, remind me," I repeat. "How do you get the money you need to invest in the companies you have, to do the work you will do and gain the contracts you need?" I feel a bit of a dampener at this point and wonder if I am getting little old for this type of thing.

I said. Just three things. Think about the future, look friendly and be strong".

"What about the clothes and looking rich?"

"Yeah, that too, like I said. Three things!"

"Right."

"I want to do the traditional things but in a new way. There is also an important thing to do. When the company is successful. We have to give back, give back to invest in it to make it more successful. Not just take the money out. I think end-to-end all the time. If I see something I challenge it and think why is that like that and why can't we make it better? I am thinking like this all the time."

"Right."

I am left breathless by the onslaught of seemingly disconnected, possibly unfunded, but undoubtedly interesting ideas from Mathew, who is a young man in a hurry. Going somewhere. I rather feel he will hit lucky somehow, someday. Probably, or at least hopefully, before he burns too much of someone else's money.

Mathew magnanimously gives way to Hao and we chat about life as a young Chinese man with wealth and famous parents. It is hard going and the gulf of the age gap doesn't help. The conversation peters out in an unsatisfactory way.

Hao is a personable, good-looking, well-dressed young man with wealth and connections as well as talent, so perhaps Mathew has already got some of his ingredients for success sorted, though I'm not sure which.

I am clearly unable to articulate the penetrating questions I have in my head and Hao is left floundering in a bog of Chinglish communications which leaves us agreeing to meet again sometime soon, with a good interpreter, preferably at least half my age. Mathew's interpretation seems a little more Mathew and a little less Hao so we part sworn friends and agree to have food together at some point. My offer to pay looks like much more of a sure run thing than some of the rest of the conversation, but I am tired. I invite 'Girl Friday' as well, but it's unclear to me if she accepts or if Mathew does so on her behalf.

# SUMMER

I feel the heat at the best of times, but Beijing in 'flaming June' is a hell-hole of the first order; 40 degrees is just unpleasant by any standard. This city of changes is beset by pollution of apocalyptic proportions for much of the year and the summer is no exception. Face masks, most useless against the smallest carbon particles, abound. The hospitals and pharmacies see a surge of complaints and clotted lungs. The smog is just plain gritty and you can taste it. This place needs a good spring clean! So do my lungs. I am escaping back to the UK! Pity the poor souls that have to suffer here 100% of the time and who it is said have a reduced life expectancy of at least ten years as a result. The untold long-term effects and damage to the young as well as the old seems a heavy price to pay for progress.

# The online entrepreneur

Juan Xiao (her English name is Betty though I prefer her Chinese name which means 'little' or 'little one') has the broadest and most beguiling of smiles. She lights up the room with it. Her eyes smile, her mouth smiles, her whole body smiles. Born in 1982, she is a product of a new generation in China, the always on, digitally savvy, internet generation. Born and bred in Beijing she sees herself as very much a Beijinger.

"Beijing is my home town," she says. "I love this place. All my family and relatives are here and all my friends. I know it is not a good place to live because of the pollution but I still like the city. It is losing some of its charm and as a local I sometimes feel we are losing our dignity and the workers are so rude and everyone is always rushing around with no care for others. It is such a shame. I feel a bit sad that it is changing and becoming less friendly and more impersonal. However, around Spring Festival most of the workers have gone back to their home towns and Beijing is left to the Beijingers, the locals, and it is lovely then. That's when I really feel it is home. The real Beijing is full of the history of our country. It is where the last emperor was, it is where most of the famous Chinese cultural sites are and there are many good things here. However, it is also a city fuelled and serviced by immigrants from all over China. Sometimes that detracts from the real Beijing but we have to accept it."

She smiles again. This time it is a smile full of wistful sadness, perhaps surprising for a young and successful woman who you might feel would relish the variety and complexity of a vibrant and diverse city. But no. She is already nostalgic for her days at school. Such is the speed of change in China and specifically Beijing that even the young can be nostalgic about their recent ~t. She shakes her head and with it dispels the nostalgia and childhood ~ries. Like many young unmarried women, Xiao lives at home. Parents will be hopeful for marriage but I sense a determination to buck those immediate expectations in favour of entrepreneurialism.

"I went to Ritan Middle School. Then, the Beijing Technology in Business University where I studied journalism. I stayed here. Now I am a Taobao entrepreneur."

Taobao has been an extraordinary success in China since it was founded in 2003. It is owned by Alibaba, which in turn set Wall Street alight with the biggest IPO in history at $25bn in September 2014. Taobao features nearly a billion products and is one of the top 20 most visited websites in the world. It is a little like eBay, with all the bells and whistles you could imagine on top. This is not the place to explain the intricacies of Taobao, but suffice to know that fortunes are made on it every day in China as ordinary people use it to buy and sell pretty much everything. Xiao is a classic user and her story serves as an example of how it has touched and changed the lives of many young Chinese people.

"I was really lucky after I left university as I worked for Wall Street English, a well-known English school in China. I worked there for five years from 2006, and in 2011 I went to New Zealand on a working holiday. I saw many interesting things and found some very interesting products there. I thought that my friends would like to hear about these products such as Mānuka honey, health products, special make up and milk powder."

She posted her views on the products online, on WeChat, the ubiquitous Chinese cross between Facebook and Twitter with video and voice communications and soon to come electronic payment thrown in. It's a common thing now for all the younger Chinese and most of the older middle class ones too. Many of her friends asked her to buy some products for them and send them back to China. So she did.

"I don't want to earn a lot of money. I want a different lifestyle from many of my friends who are always so stressed and busy, bound to their work. People started asking me to send products and then they posted on WeChat that the products were good, so more people, who I didn't know and who were just reading about the products, started to make contact and ask me to ship products to them too."

Starting small, Xiao now has more than 400 regular customers across China for these specialist and very New Zealand products.

"The quality is very good and I get great reviews online, so it seems people want to buy more and more".

She smiles at me. A modest but clearly very proud smile. It is heart melting and speaks of Xiao's warm and honest approach which seems both to emanate from and permeate the products she sells, as well as the style in which she does it.

"I decided I did not want to work in Beijing. It is polluted and the subway is so crowded. It is mayhem at rush hour and people rush to work and spend a long time doing it and getting home, for what? A bit more money. I didn't want that. It is easy to trade products and I can manage my time well during the day so it leaves me with time to go out, to talk to people, to do interviews!"

That melting smile again. This is a very determined young woman and her smile belies the determination and focus her actions show. She has limited ambition for the business and it seems something of a means to an end to allow her to do something extraordinary.

"I want to go to a poor area of China and teach poor children; maybe Sichuan province, in Xi Chang city. I have a friend who did that and spent three months there. She found it so very rewarding and I want to do something like that. Maybe to teach the children English."

This is unusual in a China populated by so many that are money-hungry, status- and face- seeking. Xiao's quiet and determined comment intrigues me but she does not elaborate on when she believes this dream will be realized.

"I get up early in the morning and call New Zealand to book and order products from my suppliers. I know exactly how long it takes to get the products to Beijing so I have to manage things carefully and guess thoughtfully about the order pipeline and likely sales timetable so I do not order too little or too much. I package products in the afternoon and then send them all off. Many customers are friends, but more and more they are friends of friends and I can't let any of them down. It is important that they can rely on me to do what I say I will, when I say I will so they will trust me, trust the products, come back for more and tell others so my business grows."

The simplicity of her approach and focus on a great product, delivered on time at a sensible price, would be the envy of many larger businesses. Unsurprisingly, people pay on time and regularly re-order.

Simple business models work.

"Taobao is a good chance for me to set up on my own. For less than ¥20,000 (£2,200) I was able to get everything set up and started. If I work efficiently and carefully, I can earn up to ¥50,000 (£5,500) a month, which is just enough."

The subject turns to women and the role of women in society. I think the question which sparked it was the standard one all young unmarried women are asked across China every day. "When will you get married?" Many have the answer ready, that they are dating and hopeful, or engaged and planning or marrying soon. Xiao has none of these answers and avoids answering altogether.

"Women in this city are much more independent. Work changes everything. If you work and have money you have independence and self-determination. You don't need a husband. They can tie you down to social norms. I know a friend who asked her husband for money to go travelling and he said no! So she got a job and started travelling! She was right to do it. He had no right to tie her down. As women become more confident and self-orientated and independent then they become more empowered and have a voice. This is very important."

The subject is one we chat about more and Xiao is clearly passionate about the importance of women in society and the home as equals. Her perspective is increasingly common among young women and there is a growing movement of women's empowerment not only in Beijing but across many of the major Chinese cities. It is still, however, a little discussed or encouraged subject in the lower Tier cities and rural communities where tradition seeps through the fabric of family and history. However, China is changing quickly and I believe the shift is more and more clear as the old formalities of family and rural life give way to the spread of urbanization and the lifting of millions of Chinese people, first out of poverty and then into the emerging middle classes with money and ambition in equal measure.

# Breaking with tradition

Celine, as she prefers to be known, is a confident and self-assured young woman. Born in Beijing in 1983, she is recently returned from two years in the UK where she completed a Masters in International Management at Royal Holloway College in the very heart of London. After a first degree in international business from the well-known Beijing Union University she first worked for a few years and then went to London and completed her Masters. She is a highly articulate woman who speaks perfect English with only the hint of a Chinese accent. She has returned to get married. Her work now is in advertising account management at a media company and her husband works for an overseas education company. They are the quintessential urbanites of China, members of the new emerging middle class of the country with a powerful blend of language, international outlook, education and money.

"I was very fortunate as I have worked in the media industry since I graduated," she says, "first in Tencent (the hugely successful competitor to Alibaba) as an advertising executive and in business development for two years in Beijing. After that, I spent almost six years in a start-up advertising company in a similar role before working for Vogue China for almost three years. Then I went to London."

Why did she return to China?

"When I was in London, I came home a few times for family reunions and of course at Chinese New Year. It was at one of these events that I met my husband. We were both at a casual dinner of family friends. Then both parents ˙reed to meet and we started what became a long distance relationship as he ˙in Beijing and I was back in London. After a year, I then decided to come ˙nd we were married recently."

Celine is proud to be a Beijinger, born and brought up in the city where she now lives.

"Beijing now is not what it used to be like when I was a child. The pace has visibly increased. But this is an important city on the world stage now. Shanghai is probably more visibly international but Beijing is the place of political power and decision making. Some people really feel that Beijing is home. They feel they belong to Beijing. We are proud of our city as it has some of the best education establishments and hospitals in China and they are of a world class standard."

So what does she see happening in the next few years?

"I guess I might have a baby in the next three years, maybe then I will be self-employed so I can look after the baby and spend more time with it. I want to set up a Chinese-UK business."

Doing what? I am curious.

Her reply is enthusiastic and clearly articulated.

"Education is the future of China, the Chinese and Chinese children. I want to set up summer schools for Chinese children to be in the UK. I want to have an education company focused on cultural exchanges. My husband and I discussed the idea and he is more experienced from his current job so he can advise me."

The idea unfolds and is as disarmingly simple as it is astute.

"When I was in the UK, I worked in a similar project so I was able to wor<sup>*</sup> with a number of UK schools. I think there is a ready market at both e<sup>*</sup> here in China with many parents with money wanting their children exposed to the international stage, and in the UK where there are with the facilities and financial needs to provide the services we would use in the long summer holidays. My husband will build the China business. I think it is a brave idea. We are going to give it a try and see if we can succeed."

Here again is that unstoppable and raw enthusiasm that you find so often in China. The attitude is, "why not?", "let's try" and "we can do it". The idea seems logical and an interesting and saleable one which UK schools could well buy into.

"My husband is a very traditional Chinese man. He likes history, Chinese opera, poetry and calligraphy. Our relationship has developed, it has just happened. I am very satisfied with how it is working out. I am particularly happy about the equality in our marriage. It is a democratic marriage. We can discuss anything and talk a lot each day about our future, where we will live, what we will do."

This is indeed a little more unusual than the old traditional way of Chinese marriage. Celine's comments say more than the words alone. That she is saying the things she is suggest something abnormal, something surprising in many other Chinese marriages. This is the new style of marriage where the woman is empowered and equal. Not tied to the children, tradition, and kitchen sink.

"The role of women in China is changing. More and more husbands are taking more and more roles in the home as more and more women take wider responsibilities at work. It used to be that women should, in the old way of thinking, have a baby, look after the home and preparation of food while being a good daughter and, specifically, a good daughter-in-law. Now, it is more like the Western society. In the bigger cities such as Beijing and Shanghai, many women choose to be at home, they are not forced to by social norms. It is a choice not an expected role."

The story of women's rights and empowerment is one explored elsewhere in this book. It is a recurring theme, which seems to have lost its old taboo. Stories of women being held back and prevented from having a wider role come flooding in across history in China and certainly there remain places where the role of women remains at best ambiguous and at worst home- and baby-bound.

now there are places such as in the south of China, such as in Guangdong, men are at the top and women are at the bottom. I have heard of villages where women are not even allowed to sit at the same table to have food with the men."

How much of this is true I am not sure, but who am I to argue. China is an enormous country, full of diversity and differences. It's quite possible that such practices exist. However, in Beijing the picture is quite different among those to whom I speak. There is a strong and growing number of women's empowerment groups which are well attended and supported. They are led by Chinese women for Chinese women, from groups struggling to raise the issues around domestic violence, another taboo subject in many cultures and no less so in China, to self-help business groups encouraging and mentoring women to take the lead in the work environment.

"Work has changed women's lifestyles and life position in China. Financial independence has been the catalyst for women's empowerment and freedom from the past."

Indeed it has and so it should, in the eyes of many, including me.

# The writer

Lijia Zhang is a writer. Having started life in a very poor family, in a very poor set of circumstances in Nanjing, she spent many of her formative years struggling in 1980s China. She worked for 16 years in the Chenguang Machinery Factory in Nanjing. A munitions factory of more than 10,000 workers, it was one of China's largest businesses.

"I hated life then. It was so boring. I taught myself English in between working. My co-workers were suspicious of my diligence and my 'reactionary' attitude. It was at the height of the reforms and it was tough going for me. I had been given my mother's job in the factory. She handed over her tools and 'iron rice bowl' of a job for life at the age of 43. I was set for life and didn't want it. I wanted to be a writer. I wrote things from the age of 14. I have kept a personal diary ever since then. I wanted to learn English and I wanted to express myself freely from a very early age. Few people encouraged me but those who did changed my life."

Her book, *Socialism is Great*, tells the fascinating story in detail but we choose to talk about her life since those momentous years when she organized the largest demonstration by Nanjing workers in support of the Tiananmen Square Protest in 1989. More than 500 protested. It was a difficult time afterwards and she was suspended from work and investigated by the authorities. However, now she has no qualms in talking about it and her past seems accepted by officialdom. She became a regular writer in both the Chinese language, as well as international press.

"I was very driven to learn English and it changed my life. I was so unhappy at the factory as I said. So when I had the chance I left China. I had to make sure that I was able to acquire the right papers and 'chop' (the stamp of authorization) from the factory. The manager was against me at that time, seeing me as a reactionary and 'decadent bourgeois element' as he suspected my naturally curly hair was because I had a perm. As a result he steadfastly refused to issue the right authorization. However, my sister had the right connections at the same factory and so we were able to get the stamps, the 'chops' I needed to leave."

She went to the UK having met a young Scottish man, Calum MacLoud, on a rare business trip to Beijing in 1988. They developed a relationship and, in 1990, Lijia was able to leave as Calum's fiancé. They married, and subsequently divorced, but she was free from the old factory life and working as a writer and occasional journalist for foreign publications.

Lijia describes her personal journey as that of a frog trapped at the bottom of a well, knowing that she could see little of the world outside, but that it was there and an interesting and colourful place, while her life was a grey and cold one. Her perspective was of a simple and boring life confined within the walls of the munitions factory, living in a small flat, attending the factory provided bathhouse, library, cinema and the poor schools available to her. Even the 'university' at which she soaked up the thin availability of knowledge from 1992 to 1995 was paid for, and within, the factory.

She writes elsewhere that mechanical engineering was hardly her preferred option but the course was her only route to any form of learning. She struggled but loved the atmosphere and the pressure of learning.

"Why did I come back to China? Well, I really felt that life was meaningful and purposeful here. I really believed I could make a difference and help tell the real stories of China. After attending a UK journalism course with a journalism school I found I could work back here as a Chinese 'fixer' for foreign reporters. I was freelancing and it became clear to me - and others - that I had a good eye for a story. I managed to get myself a full-time job with a US broadcasting company, working in both radio and television."

"Unfortunately I was, and guess I still am, quite opinionated. I end~ being offered a job working for a competitor, which I couldn't do s~

regulations forbid, and still forbid, Chinese nationals to work as reporters for foreign media owners. You can be an assistant or researcher, but you couldn't and can't write for them."

She wrote for the competitor and got published outside China. Her employers found out, and she was out.

"I became a researcher for Newsweek, and in September 1996, I went freelance as a journalist based here in China but writing for overseas publications. It was the best decision I ever made. I was then able to right OpEds (opinion editorials, where the author is not affiliated to a publication but writes for them) for newspapers such as The Guardian and The Observer in the UK as well as others across the world and in South Asia."

"These are not so sensitive and I only write in English. Those days in the factory when I was driven to hiding my English books and secretly reading them during political meetings, really helped me acquire a rich vocabulary. I was laughed at by my co-workers and publicly humiliated by my boss when he discovered what I was doing, but it made all the difference."

So what are her favourite topics for the writing she does now?

"Society is changing in China and that's the topic I find fascinating. Social mobility, the immense income gap between the rich and the poor. The rich are getting richer and the poor are substantially lagging behind, despite the reforms and undeniable improvements. I can't really see any major change to this situation in the next 10 years either. The best universities are populated by the brightest kids, but the brightest kids are those with the best education and the best education is afforded to those with the money to pay for it. The rich can afford the best education for their kids and in this society of the one child, the kids are the 'emperors' and the doted favourites of the family. They want for nothing and though the pressure to perform is high, so are the opportunities."

Who are the underprivileged? The ethnic minorities? The migrant workers?

"There are many people on the margins of society. The famous awarding of the Hukou (the residency papers determining where you live in China) developed ↄ the 1950s was really to stop the poor flooding to the growing cities. The ҡou keeps the poor in the villages. Under this system people from outside ⸱ties can't come to own property inside. The city folk still enjoy huge and ⸱ortionate privileges. There are moves by the government to change this but it is slow going. For example, there has been a relaxing of the laws recently that mean the children of migrant works who have lived in Beijing for five years, are now eligible to attend city schools."

The topic of the migrant workers has fascinated me ever since I first came to China and we divert our conversation to explore this underclass further.

"The migrant workers in China are the unsung heroes of the economic miracle of China. There are realistically two classes in Beijing: the migrants and the indigenous Beijingers. The government is addressing the inequalities, but the locals jealously guard their privileges and exalted status."

I have personally observed little elements of this privilege in the city's parks and public places where card-holding locals wander in free of charge, while the foreigners, including migrant workers and those from outside the city, pay.

"I see myself as someone who can provide a cultural bridge between China and the West."

We are discussing our respective roles and jobs.

"In 2008 I was a strong and vocal supporter of China hosting the Olympics."

"Why?"

"Because China needed – and still needs – to engage with the West. It was, for too long, in the shadows or perceived to be. There are so many freedoms here now. The cage is so big that most people almost don't notice it is there. They can't feel the limits at all. It's only those who push the envelope that feel the edges."

Of course, the edges are there but even when people bump against them, sometimes unwittingly, the edges become the butt of jokes as well as WeChat and internet ridicule. There is not much the government can do to stop people complaining any more. There are ways around the firewalls and the sheer volume of internet traffic means that it is almost impossible to curb it, even if the government wanted to do so totally, of which absolute intent I am personally dubious. There is enough pride and sense of personal improvement in the people to warrant outright dissent over many of th' issues of the day. Pollution, poorly enforced law, inefficient or incompet' policing and political ineffectuality are pilloried. The flood of comr' which occupy the popular background noise on WeChat, and the othe' networks, probably serves to bolster, rather than hinder or obstruct, the official preferences to root out graft and incompetence.

The last words go to Lijia

"Any country that can, on the one hand censor the amount of flesh shown by an actress playing the last great empress Cixi, and on the other allow netizens the seemingly absolute freedom to ridicule the stupidity of the post production censorship, has my vote. The place is changing and although it may seem slow, even glacial at times, it is a change of inexorable dimensions. No one can hold the Chinese people back any more."

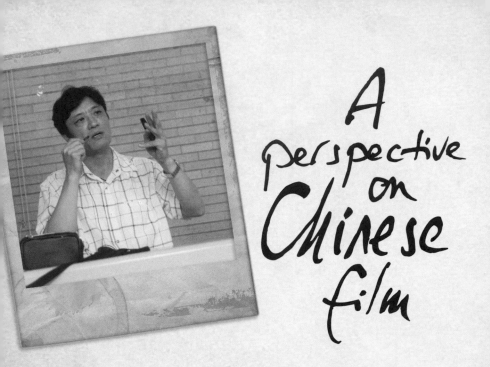

# A perspective on Chinese film

Professor Huang Yingxia is President of the Beijing Film Academy (BFA), the only film academy in China and the largest in Asia. He is waiting for me. A wiry and intense man with a shock of black hair, he has lived through and significantly influenced, the changing face of the Chinese film industry.

China is now the world's fastest-growing film market, with a feature film being released into this enormous market at a rate of nearly two a day. Box office receipts in 2014 ran to ¥29.6bn (£3.19bn) which made it the second-largest film market after the US, globally. The industry began in 1896 and the first Chinese film, The Battle of Dingjunshan, was made in 1905.

Professor Huang explains: "I was born in 1959 and was at primary school in Western Beijing during the Cultural Revolution. I remember that the school had no glass in the windows and no desks or chairs to start with. We had to bring our own stool from home to sit on. The blackboard was a painted section of the wall on which the teacher used chopsticks to scratch lessons. It was primitive and I distinctly remember the very first thing we learned was how to say "Long live Chairman Mao". It's a very strong memory from my first day as a naive seven year old at primary school. I remember those days were difficult and there were different groups of people fighting each other in the fields and surrounding area".

...ssor Huang is there. His eyes grip mine in an intensity of memory, ...holds the attention like a vice.

"I remember we had to put newspaper over the windows and then a felt and cotton curtain in winter to keep out the cold. Also, in the winter, we had no electricity so school started and ended with the light. I thought that was normal life. There were about 40 or maybe 50 children in the class. Then around Grade 5, I recollect they put glass in the windows but there were still no lights and no electricity in the school."

While this sounds harsh, I have spoken to many Chinese people of this generation who remember just the same and worse conditions in the schools they attended. Some had endured rooms lacking doors and sometimes schools were almost outside as semi-covered structures stuck on the end of otherwise unprepossessing buildings, housing a local machine tool shed, barn or shop.

"We had a stove in the winter to help us keep warm," continues Professor Huang. Each child had to take turns to go in early to set up the stove in the winter so the room was at least a little less cold when class started. In our third year we were given a desk and a chair, though they were not new but old, well-used ones."

"Middle school was a dream by comparison. We had electric light and glass in the windows. I also vividly remember that the classroom had a proper blackboard. It felt like a real school."

Professor Huang's father was a coal miner working in the local pit while his mother worked in the personnel department at the mine.

"My father was responsible for the pit mine shaft lift. It was a very important job."

There then followed a day remembered by all of Professor Huang's generation with a vividness that is both compelling and telling.

"It was in the second year of my high school: 9 September, 1976. We were all called into the playground at the sudden order of the principal. There were loud speakers round the square and a solemn announcement of the death of Chairman Mao. We all cried. It was a very genuine outpouring of real emotion. I remember that moment very well. I remain astonished looking back that everyone felt like that."

Official histories tell the official stories but the reality at the grass roots of society was an outpouring as heartfelt and shocking as those that touched the hearts of Americans at the assassination of J F Kennedy and the British day Princess Diana died.

"1977 was the year that enrolment was announced for university entrance examinations. We were delighted. We all worked hard to pass the exams. The score required was 265 for those at high school and 310 for those of us at middle school. I got 307. So I failed! I had to wait another year to try again and then in 1978 I passed. I was entered in to the BFA. My entrance into the world of film was entirely accidental. I heard that the BFA would take students for the very first time. I played the violin at the time and my tutors said it was a good idea to try to get into something artistic! I listened to them and became one of the first intake to the Academy of the post-Cultural Revolution generation."

Huang fell into the sound recording department and has been there ever since. He rose to become Head of Sound and then Dean. Save for a period, which began in 1982 with 'his despatch', the BFA has been Huang's life. The 'despatch' was the time when students graduated they were sent to the provinces. As he then explained, it was a tortuous and difficult time with luck and timing of the changes around Deng Xiaoping playing a critical role in his fortunes.

"Every province had a film studio for propaganda purposes. I was sent to Hunan province and stayed there for six years, mainly filming. I was the sound man on the classic film of the time, The Great Parade. There were famous directors such as Wu Ziniu making films then. The films were shot without sound and then the soundtrack was added afterwards, with the censor's permission."

We discuss the role of the censor at the time and the undoubted strictures and constraints that were imposed. It was undoubtedly a difficult time in the nascent industry, but an exciting one too as it emerged from the dark days of the Cultural Revolution.

Huang was based in the county of Changshan and, as such, his Hukou (or resident permit) was issued there, rather than in his home in Beijing. In those days, as now, once you were given a Hukou that was it. You were destined to remain where you were placed for ever. It would determine your future and the future of your descendants, where they could have education, get married and live.

"There was only one way to get back to Beijing and to the academy. I needed to be a graduate student back in Beijing and to get my Hukou ''redespatched''. really struggled but managed to do it and in 1988 I was 'redespatched' to ng. So there I was, back at the BFA. You had to follow all the formalities did, and by abiding by the strict rules, I was able to graduate only in the second year of accredited graduates from the academy. The first year was 1977 - 1981 and my intake of 1978 - 1982, was the second. The generation of 1981 and 1982 was a very strictly controlled one for the despatch. However, after 1985, the rules gradually loosened more and more so by 1990/91, when I eventually graduated in the post graduate school, the despatch was not so strict and I managed to stay at BFA in the sound department as a teacher."

Huang's story is unusual, his timing could be said to be perfect, or maybe just incredibly lucky, since 1986 was the first year that students were allowed to graduate from, as opposed to just finish, their studies and be sent home, or to a pre-determined role. In 1988, the sound department of BFA was allowed to graduate students and he was therefore in the right place at the right time to do so. He became one of the first generation of students to be classed as true, certified, graduates.

"I did not know when the authorities at the academy would be allowed to issue graduation certificates. But I guessed it would be soon so I just gambled on being lucky and prepared hard. I started to learn English and hung around film crews in the hope of being noticed. We first filmed without syncing sound in to the process. Before the revolution there had been sound syncing but it all stopped during the Revolution as the censors would review the scripts and we would dub in the appropriate dialogue and sound effects later. It wasn't until 1985 that we were allowed to film and sound-sync simultaneously. It was a big debate at the time around how film and sound should be filmed in reality. Of course, the film teams believed we should film and sync sound to be real but the censors didn't agree for many years. Even after the Cultural Revolution, the scripts were reviewed and approved before we could film and develop material 'in reality'."

The change brought on a revolution in filming. During the Cultural Revolution, there were no films imported in to China so the developments of Hollywood and Western film techniques never touched the Chinese industry.

"To be honest, we had no idea about how to sync sound. We just had no experience. Gradually, real sound was reintroduced to film tracks. The first ever film to have this was made in 1988 by Yie Shan called Wild Mountain. It was awarded the Golden Cock Award. It was a defining moment in Chinese film-making."

Huang eventually rose to become the Dean of the Graduate Scho BFA. He continued to learn English, and in 1996, he had his first ch go to America.

"In the March and April of that year I was using and browsing the internet. It was early days and I actually got through to the West. I had an old desktop and a telephone modem beside it. I browsed USC (the University of Southern California) and saw an email address there. I just took a bet and sent an email to that address, totally out of the blue. I asked about their film curriculum."

To Huang's total astonishment he had a reply. It seemed that there then followed a series of halting and sporadic emails. Huang took a chance and asked if there would be any interest in USC either sending someone over to Beijing to deliver lectures about the US film industry or invite someone from the emerging Chinese industry, Huang, to go to the US. The take-up was almost immediate, it seems, and Huang was invited. He then had to get his boss to agree and to raise the money to fund the visit. June that year found him flying to the US and meeting the person to whom he had sent the speculative email.

"It turned out that the guy I had emailed was the head of sound at USC. It was wonderful to be able to have the opportunity to meet him and to learn what was happening in the US industry. Better still, we were able to get him to come back over to Beijing. He lectured for five days and we arranged two days sight-seeing as well."

It appeared that the visit was a great success and the relationship with USC has persisted ever since those early days. The head of sound at USC subsequently reported on the visit to the Dean, and in 1997, the Dean visited the BFA.

"She came and said that my language skills were good enough to lecture at USC. So I was able to spend a year there teaching students. The class was known as the '3/10' class and became a very famous production class in the history of the USC undergraduate school. I went with my wife and she undertook research on Chinese films, also at USC. Before the mid-1990s directors were from the fifth generation of Chinese film. They all grew up in the old traditions. We knew we couldn't just throw away the old ideas, but we had new ones of our own too."

Huang explains the 'generations' of Chinese film makers. He belonged to the famous 'sixth generation' which followed the generation which had pioneered, and created greater interest in, Chinese films abroad. There were films as Red Sorghum (1987), The Story of Qiu Ju (1992) and Farewell My Concubine (1993).

ns of the pre-1989 era were of the traditional emotions, family and the of the generations. After the mid-1990s it was a new generation (6th) of Chinese film with a more Western feel to them. Films switched a lot to meet the international culture and tastes. The old generations' influence became less and less. Our generation has a culture to encourage people to be positive and to grow. We consider films to be an element to influence the people's feelings. The government still wants all films to be a tool of propaganda about positive living, but it is also what the cinema goers are demanding so both are in sync."

Chinese films are now winning awards. The recent Silver Bear Award at the 2014 Berlin International Film Festival was given to Chinese-made Black Coal Thin Ice and more are expected.

Huang explains why he believes the awards are now coming thick and fast.

"There has been a refocusing by directors on specific people and the individual rather than the general story or a group of characters. This is becoming a more accepted approach as the big directors take a stand on this new style."

I ask: "With so many films released each year can they all make money?"

"Frankly, no they can't. You just can't make big money from the non-popular films, even though some directors want to make films in this new individual focused style. Comedy certainly sells in China. Thai Tour about three guys on holiday in Thailand and To our Youth are both comedy films with a more retrospective style which have tapped into the nostalgia of youth culture and the golden years of youth."

Huang is one of the most experienced professors on Chinese film and his encyclopaedic knowledge is a product of his history and personal experience of having lived through, and significantly influenced, the development of the Chinese film industry. Today, he says, it is essential to be able to "read society", to be able to bet on the next big wave of social consciousness, which will fuel successful and big box office hits. There is still rapid change in the economy, culture and emotional engagement of the people and this needs to be delicately and carefully anticipated.

"It is a very dynamic market. One day it is one thing and the next it is something else. This means that the film industry is very dynamic. Indeed, the young students can be very successful if they hit the top of a culture wave. However, you also films crash and burn. There was a recent case where the predictions were ¥1.0 bn (£110m) box office hit but on release it only did around ¥0.5 bn (£ about 50% of the prediction. You don't make money when that happen'

"The industry has to guess the audience's taste even before they might actually have it. It is a nightmare for the industry and the investors."

It seems as if the small investors are being left behind as the larger, increasingly international ones, from the US, Hong Kong, Taiwan and even France, are taking a broader bet on a series of projects and accepting low returns on some, in the hope of a windfall on others. There are signs of individuals, as well as institutions, backing Chinese film. Huang explains that some savvy investors are providing seed funding to student directors and small production houses to get an international award which will catapult them to fame. Then, on the back of the award, the next film from the director can gross huge returns on the back of a much lower, 'made you famous', contract. Here, the student or young director pretty well seems to sell their soul for the fame and give up the returns to the investors. But then it is their choice and everyone wants to be famous in this industry. It is not populated by the shy, retiring types.

"What is your prediction for the future of the Chinese film industry and cinema goers here?"

"When I look forward, I think there is still room to make money. 3D and the new sound systems will bring new techniques and also new audience experiences that will make money. There are big developments in sound, films like Gravity and Interstellar have been enormous successes in China as well as globally. The Chinese don't make SciFi movies and they have stolen some share here. Comedy will certainly work well into the future in my mind. The retrospective theme film will also be successful. Talking about when people were growing up, the sky was blue and the grass was green. This will continue to touch the hearts of the Chinese cinema goer and a large segment of the population. So millions will flock to watch these sorts of stories and millions will be made on the back of them."

"In the 1980s, the stories were straightforward and just clear from one end to the other. Now the stories are much more filmic. Now they have layers on layers and the shots must be more complex, the films are more technically difficult and creative. The demand of the audience is much more complex, much more open-minded. The changes in the industry are a metaphor of China and have been a mirror of the changes in China."

"In the past, movies were used for propaganda and educative purposes. Now they are more pure entertainment. Of course, the stories have some ...ance, to teach the people something of a moral lesson, but they have ...in first."

As in the history of many countries, the Chinese state historically used film as a tool for promulgating the government agenda. The medium was also used to educate the population and there were strict guidelines to ensure story lines were patriotic, had happy endings and a moral core.

Huang's life mirrors that of both the Chinese film industry and China's recent history. The story of film has changed dramatically in China as has Huang's life. I feel that I have been the recipient of one of the best ever lectures on the history of the Chinese film industry. I am sure there are millions of words written on the subject, but to hear it first-hand, from the mouth of one of the most celebrated leaders in the industry, has been an education and a privilege.

# Marriage and women's empowerment

Lanna Wu is unusual. She is from Inner Mongolia, from the steel-producing and polluting provincial capital city of Hohhot. She speaks perfect English with a confidence and poise that makes you forget it is her second, if not third, language. She speaks Chinese and was also taught Mongol as a child. She was born in 1981. She is unmarried, by choice, and resolutely refusing to marry someone her parents think is suitable. "I will find the person I want to marry for love, not for society."

Lanna moved to Beijing in 2000 to complete her first degree in English and International Trade. Then she went to the UK in 2004 and spent time with several UK companies ending up as a project manager for the Greater London Authority.

"I wanted to do an MA, so attended The London School of Economics and got it in social policy and development. It took a year and then I worked for a consulting company for a year looking at Asia strategies for business. I only ̣ad a postgraduate Visa, so could only stay in the UK for two years but I'm ̣ I did."

̣id you come back to Beijing rather than go home?"

"My parents suggested that I work for the government back home, but I went home for a month and really didn't see myself working for government. There was also huge peer pressure."

"For what?"

"To get married, conform, fit in. It is a lot less in Beijing. But at home there is pressure from my parents and a wider pressure on them from the locals and friends. I came to Beijing and now work for the European Chamber of Commerce as a business manager. My role is in helping overseas companies lobby the Chinese government and to help them understand the Chinese market."

"What do you think is going to happen with overseas companies entering China?"

# "I will find the person I want to marry for love, not for society."

"It is going to be harder and harder for companies to enter China. The big companies are already quite localized. They know how to play by the rules. After 2008 (the global financial crisis), people think that China is the big market opportunity but costs are escalating here so companies are changing their priorities. They are going to other Asian countries. I see the opportunities in China are for the Chinese corporates."

Lanna feels that the state-owned enterprises (SOEs) of China have the biggest chance to grow on the back of the expanding middle classes and the explosion of increased financial security many millions of Chinese now feel.

"Foreign-owned companies have two choices. They can wait and see what happens and grow with the market. Or they can work with existing companies in joint ventures. The market is going to be controlled here and people have to accept that is how it is. Oversees companies will lose patience and go elsewhere. They can't afford to wait for ever. For consumer products, China is a market, not a production centre. They can make product elsewhere more cheaply now and then import."

Lanna is impressively knowledgeable and articulate about her work I sense there is something else that drives this woman.

"What do you do when you are not working for money?"

Her face lights up, I've hit the right nerve.

"In my spare time I am the Chapter Leader of the Beijing branch of the Marco Polo Institute. It was founded by a group of French nationals and we have about 200 people. It provides a platform for young business people to learn more about China. We have regular presentations and share experiences. We publish an annual report and are a think tank really. I know the founder of the Beijing Chapter and he left Beijing to work overseas and he asked me to take over the role of leading the Beijing Chapter."

Lanna is a torrent of words and energy, unquestionably passionate about the work of the Institute.

"My day job is the heavy stuff. I really think a lot about how I can contribute to making China a better place. I like the fact that the Institute is about us all being equals in thinking together about problems and finding practical solutions. I really like the spirit of debate at the Institute. I want to apply my knowledge to help society. No one wants to talk about social policy, but at Marco Polo we all share the debate to learn about the important issues facing us. I really want to be a public policy adviser and Marco Polo is really helping me better understand the issues."

Can you give me some examples of the issues you feel need addressing?

"There is no social pressure through work to get married. They don't care if I am married or not. However, a friend of mine who works at a large SOE told me that she has been told that she can't be promoted as she is not married and so cannot be mature! I have friends who are married and many who are not. Most of the girls I know who are not married are working for foreign companies. Foreign companies not only allow you to be you, with no pressure on marriage or meeting the other social norms, but they also give good holidays."

The Chinese business approach to holidays is legendary. You are usually allowed five days plus one day a year. You have to make up the national holidays by working the following weekend usually. I have written elsewhere in these Notes about holidays but it bears repeating that the Chinese are instructed when holidays are to be taken as defined by the government and if they take more they need express permission and it is usually unpaid.

"So many of my friends who work for government or SOEs see no future in their work. They just turn up and show their face. The attitude of the bosses is parental. There is not much incentive to grow and develop."

"What about your parents? What do they think about your approach to life, not being married and working for a foreign business?"

"I am financially independent. I don't really let my parents have control of my life. They are ok with that. Now. My dad was ok from early on but my mum is still always on edge about it."

"About what?"

"She is trying to match-make for me all the time. She wants me to be happy, but I know what she really wants, which is for me to be stable, and to her, that means married with children. She is always finding eligible men. They have a good job, a Hukou (the residency permit). She never considers if they have hobbies, what they are like as people. My mum says that doesn't matter. What matters is the stability. I tell her that I'm not on the shelf of a supermarket. Mum often cries when we speak or meet. She thought I was wrong to go to the UK. She said it was the worst thing I could ever have done but I know it was the best thing I could ever have done for me."

This topic is the central nerve of family discord and the spinal column of tradition in China. I have met young men and women who have felt forced to 'tick the box' and move on. Love is often not at the heart of marriage but the craving for stability that their parents have on their behalf in a society that has seen so little for so long. The increased number of divorces is said to be a product of the recent changes in Chinese society and the battle of the generations, between tradition and a new culture of financial independence and increased choice for the young, emerging middle class.

Lanna is among a small, yet growing, minority of women who seek wider and greater empowerment.

"I am in control of me," she says. "For many people, marriage is about stability, being cared for when you are old as you will have children to do so but I want to find a partner who shares by beliefs and feelings. Many guys I meet are just partly looking for a box to be ticked. The social pressures are very significant. It is a competitive environment and marriage is on the 'to do' list."

She pauses, deep in thought for a moment, then plunges on into the thick the subject.

"No one seems to think about the reality of marriage. I have many divorced friends. They married because they felt they had to and then became desperately unhappy. I see the struggle with many successful women I know. They feel they can't be a good wife, mother, daughter, worker, leader. There are those who have seen a wider perspective and have a husband who believes they are equals and shared the housework and the like. They are a different and empowered breed. They have a very different view.

"Even if you get married to a foreigner you will still be subject, as a woman, to pressure from parents expecting children within a year and then for them to be fully involved in bringing up your children, not to mention actually living with you all the time to do so."

She looks at me to check I am not looking bemused or judging her in some way. I am doing neither. I have lived here too long and heard this story too often. It should be told.

"I face the same challenges as women across China. It's just that different people have different coping mechanisms. I am also a Chinese Mongolian. I am not Han (the majority race of China). I did try to learn the language but really failed. So I am an outsider in Mongolia as I speak Mandarin and an outsider in the rest of China as I have a Mongolian face. I am in the middle."

"And how does that feel?"

"Some days it is good and I feel proud and some days it is bad and I feel frustrated. Beijing people are quite narrow-minded as being born and growing up here means that they never really learned about anywhere else. Beijing is the centre of the world for them. They have the Beijing Hukou and life is easier for them. When you are from outside then you have to work harder to get what and where you want to be. It's not a problem for me. People choose jobs if they can get a Hukou on the back of it but I believe that career choice should not be made by the need for a Hukou. I am relatively choosy to follow my own life choices. I believe that if I am capable, then I will be able to work out the problems and a way round them."

"Will you get married and have a baby?"

"Yes, I hope so, but for love not for society. If I have a baby then I will certainly ave to send them for education to Inner Mongolia as that is where my Hukou ut I don't worry about that."

"And in five years' time? Where do you think you will be?"

"I want to be as happy then as I am right now. I like me and I want to be able to make choices on my own reason and views. I really don't have a plan as such. I don't see my parents often and I want to build my life now so if I have to go and look after them in the future I will have had a good life.

"I have a brother who is younger than me, he is 30 and lives not far from my parents so they see him often. That is good for them. I just can't go back too often with my job and my life choice. Every single woman in China suffers from the guilt of knowing they will have to look after their parents when they are older. Of course, I have to go home at Chinese New Year but there is lots of pressure then. A lot of my cousins are already married, so I am always in big trouble when I go home. I have to just sit and listen to everyone asking me why I am not married, when will I get married, am I seeing someone. I know it is their way of showing they care about me but it is very difficult. I don't care personally but of course I care about my parents and how they feel they are losing face to have an unmarried 30-something daughter. Every New Year I have to start the year with all the same questions. People only ask because it is the only common ground they can find with me since I am the outsider in almost every other respect. The older generation only ask me because they are concerned, they see it as a failure if you are not married, it is a social stigma."

"Aren't things changing as the new generation comes to terms with urbanization and increased affluence and choice?"

"I don't really see it. One generation is following the other. When I am home I have a role to play. Even my parents don't understand me. I have to play the role of contrite daughter who is struggling to marry. I have to play the role to shorten the distance between them and me. For me, I try not to see myself as Mongolian but rather as Lanna Wu."

She looks directly at me. A determined and defiant look. "I am me!" she declares.

I nod. What else can I do?

"Life is tough but it is tough for everyone. I see a lot of women who are still in a tough position. Women struggle with the traditional role. I would love to see women stand up and push for more equality but I don't see that in many of my married friends."

Does she know of some of the women empowerment groups in Beijing? She shakes her head so I give her the details of one group of very like-minded single Chinese and foreign women. My heart goes out to her. She is quite emotional but she is incredibly strong-willed and determination is tight across her face. Pursed lips and a furrowed brow precede her final comments. Her voice is at first strong but trembles as she continues.

# "The longer you live in China as an educated woman, the more you realize you have no power."

She addresses me directly: "The longer you live in China as an educated woman, the more you realize you have no power." she says, fixing me in a gaze I am unable to break. "You feel powerless. People like me feel they can't do anything to break the situation. It is fundamentally always seen to be the government's problem, not a personal one. People say it's for the government to do this, it's for the government to do that' but I don't agree. It is for people to take personal responsibility to create and affect change. We have a disempowered population, but that's not the government's fault that is the people themselves. They do not push for the change in society that they crave. China remains 100% male dominated. People do not want to engage as, ironically, they think it will make them even more powerless."

She slumps forward. She is exhausted by the emotion of it all. Her voice is weak now. She is weary and so am I. Time to stop this. What can I say? "Thank you" seems inane and flippant. This is a subject of such depth and of such emotion I find myself personally unable to think straight about it.

Lanna has challenged my perceptions of China and of my own society, which at times seems little better in many ways in the area of women's empowerment.

She sighs and stands up, regaining her poise and self-belief as she does. "Thank you. It was a pleasure meeting you."

"Likewise," I mumble.

# The regional manager

Lv Zhong Shan is early.

"I quit my job so I have a little more time now," he says.

This was not the introduction I had expected. In arranging the interview, never an easy thing with any Chinese person, I had been led to believe that this 31-year-old senior regional manager from BYD, the Chinese vehicle company, was a very busy man. Flexible due to his regional and mobile role, but busy.

"I was, until very recently, but I have quit my job so I can go to the California Lutheran University to do a one-year MBA. I leave Beijing on Thursday."

I am genuinely taken aback. You are not staying for New Year? It is almost unheard of for any Chinese person not to spend Chinese New Year with their family (this year it is on 19 February and we are speaking on the 9 February).

"Actually I am going back to my home town to see my mother first before I go to California."

I have to say I am a little relieved to hear this. He can see I am somewhat perplexed, so this earnest bespectacled and clean-cut man expands.

"I was working for BYD company and had done so for seven years. BYD is becoming more and more international. Last year I was supposed to be promoted but the company human resources department told me that they need people who have overseas degrees and that they were promoting a younger guy instead. He has an overseas degree. I was really upset. I really couldn't stand it so I decided it was time to go and study abroad."

I am always both impressed and not a little surprised at the way Chinese can deal with bad news. It is a culturally ingrained defence mechanism, I believe, born out of centuries of collective and continual shared hardship as well as individual suffering. There is an innate and inbuilt stoicism that seems to carry them through even the most stressful and emotionally painful experiences. Zhong Shan could have just complained about his situation and blamed the business, the system, the other guy, the internal politics and myriad other 'not me' scapegoats as so often a Westerner would, faced with the same situation. But he did not. He went out and applied for and got a place at a university the other side of the world, which he will fund at his own expense, to get a qualification he believes, but is not certain, will give him the stepping stone he needs to move up the career ladder.

"I have always had a dream to study abroad," he says. "Maybe this [being overlooked for promotion] was the sign I needed. Fate intervened in my life at the right time. The two things, my dream and my desire to progress, came together at the right time. I talked with my manager and with the human resources department. They both told me that if I get the degree then I will be able to go back to work at BYD. But maybe I will not choose to do that. Maybe I will be able to get another chance to work elsewhere in this growing and developing new energy car sector."

How can he afford to leave his job for a year and pay for the flights, the accommodation, the fees, the living expenses?

"Well I did work for seven years at BYD and I was a senior regional manager up until recently."

He seemed a little surprised at the question. The truth is that this man has been saving. In the West, mortgages and everyday life expenses drain the average household of either their entire income or usually, more than their entire income, so they are living on debt. The Chinese are savers. Recent data shows that on average Chinese workers will save up to 50% of their monthly income. Often it is more. As a result, they are buffered, though not always immune from, the vagaries of catastrophe. Most married, and many unmarried, Chinese adults will own a house outright, without a mortgage. Living expenses can be minimal if you are careful. Zhong Shan is no exception. He has managed to build up enough savings to afford this year-long 'sabbatical'. He also has managed to put a down payment on a rather nice apartment in Beijing, but more of that later.

"I was born in Shandong province in a small town called Shouguang on 10 October 1983. My Hukou is there. My father had his own business. Shandong is famous in China for its vegetables and my father was a vegetable distributor, helping local farmers get their produce to markets all over China."

He pauses. I sense the loss.

"I am sorry."

"It's ok. Thanks"

He gathers himself.

"My mother used to work for China Unicom, the big mobile phone and telephone company. She retired early and is now at home helping my married sister with her first baby. I am going home to see them for New Year."

Wrapped up in this one sentence is the whole of Chinese life. The hard-working father, a self-made man, surviving the Cultural Revolution. The working wife, now widow, dedicated first to her family and now to her grandchild. Everyone living together under the same roof, probably a small roof at that. Savings buffer the loss of the father, while marriage secures the future of the daughter. The focus is on the education of, and building the future for, the only son. Festivals, and Chinese New Year are the most important, are at the heart of family life and family is at the heart of everything. Chinese families are the security blanket that the Western world no longer seems to have. Without the, some Chinese would say, 'laziness-inducing', reliance on the Western welfare system, the Chinese are focused on self-created security, no matter how stretched and stressed they may be. As can be read elsewhere in these Notes, the price can be very high, but financial and emotional security is hard won and not given up without the greatest of struggles.

"I am a very traditional Chinese guy. My home town was the birthplace of Confucius. The people in my home town and my province are among the most traditional in China. I want to spend time with my family, I believe strongly in the Confucius teaching and in fate and I always listen to the opinion and advice of my parents."

"At 18 years old, I went to university in Chongqing, then to Shenzhen in Guangdong province. I studied electronic information engineering so I went to BYD (a large non state-owned Chinese car manufacturer) in Shenzhen. I applied for, and got, a job as an engineer for two years before I got the chance to move to a sales role as a manager. I was lucky as, not long after that, I was able to get a transfer and promotion to Beijing as the regional sales manager for Beijing and Hubei province. There are around 13 dealerships in Beijing and about 30 in Hubei province. That was in 2009. I was responsible for managing the dealerships across the area. I had to look at, and agree, working practices and policies as well as sales and marketing and advertising."

"When I started, there were about 30 people based in Beijing, but in 2011, it was widely acknowledged that BYD went in the wrong direction. They had a strategic plan but it all went too quickly and was unsustainable. Now there are only five people, I guess only four now since I have left. I was responsible for the team. BYD decided to restructure and go a bit slower to achieve their long term goals."

Zhong Shan is obviously very proud of the business and enthuses about the "best new-energy automotive company in China".

"Tesla has been successful and invested significantly in new technologies and the new energy segment of the industry but BYD is a leader. It is going to be very successful in the future."

There is no doubting his enthusiasm, or his knowledge of his industry. This is a bright and ambitious man. But why California and why the Lutheran University?

"I did apply to Peking and to Tianjin Universities and although I got an interview I could not go. These are the most difficult universities in China to get into and the tuition fees alone are over ¥300,000 (£32,800) a year. I applied to California. It is a good place and my friends said I would be happy there. Also, the weather is very nice. I got the place and also a year study Visa too so I am going to go. I have my personal savings and my mother has helped me too as she has savings."

"I chose the Lutheran University because I had heard about it first from my friends. I then went online and looked. I needed somewhere I could get a

MBA in a year. I can't afford to take any longer, either financially or from a career perspective. It fits all my criteria. A one-year MBA, a good programme and relatively cheap tuition fees."

Wrapped up in these comments are deep insights into 'the Chinese way'. With the world to choose from where does an aspiring and ambitious young man look to develop himself and expand his chances for advancement? First his family. Second his friends. Zhong Shan's personal commitment of time and money, along with the 'loan' from his mother, will provide the financial security to make the trip and fund the year, but his friends have been instrumental in the decision to go to California. He has several people he knows who are Chinese American and American Chinese (both quite different), as well as Chinese friends who are already there. A ready-made social circle will welcome him. This notion of an extended and ready-made 'family' abroad is enough to swing the decision to the broad location. Subsequently online research and dogged determination in the application process make up the rest of the jigsaw of temporary emigration.

"I started to buy my own apartment in Beijing last year. Since I am 31 years old and not married yet, I decided to put the deposit down on a new-build. It will be finished next year so the timing will work for me. I felt that if I didn't do it now then I may never do it."

Again, an insight into Chinese life and specifically marriage. An unmarried 31-year-old man without a house is not even going to get on the shortlist of most eligible urban, or many rural, girls. The expectation is that the husband will do his duty, or his family will, to buy the couple a house to live in. No mortgage, no debt. Security again plays the most important consideration, even above love, for marriage.

However, my own knowledge of buying a house in Beijing cannot stop me from posing a rather unusually direct question.

"How can you buy a house in Beijing when your Hukou is in Shouguang? You can't buy here unless you have a Beijing Hukou. How did you get round that problem?"

Zhong Shan smiles. He is happy to share the inside track and educate this foreigner in something I don't know.

"Of course everyone wants to live in the city. But not everyone can do so. It is very difficult to afford the very high prices and, of course, the regulations around people's Hukou forbid many from doing so. However, there are two types of property in Beijing. The first is called 'zhu zhai'. For this you are right. You must have a Beijing Hukou, or have lived here for at least five years. Housing is very expensive and the prices have been rising in Beijing and Shanghai, despite the slowdown elsewhere in the housing and real estate market. The lease is for 70 years as you know."

(I did not.)

"The second is newer. Some properties are in mixed use developments, so there may be a shopping mall, business offices and residential homes for sale in the same place. These are available for 50 year leases and are called 商住两用 (Shang Zhu Liang Yong). It is this type of house I have put the first payment on."

Such types of property have been around for a while in Beijing and ownership was theoretically open to all – under a local rule that meant certain developments can be used as a place to both live and from which to conduct business. The literal translation is 'apartment that can be used for residence and business'. However with the various recent changes in property ownership policies, this is now one of the few properties non–Beijingers can own in the city.

Our conversation returns to the new challenge of the next year.

"I will live on the campus. I know I will be able to look after myself when I am over there. After living in Beijing and away from home for so long I have no problem managing my daily life. Also my English has improved over the past couple of years. I have really tried hard to develop my spoken English. Although my generation did not learn English until the sixth grade at school (it is now taught from much earlier in schools) I lacked the confidence to actually speak it as I really didn't mix with foreigners very much. I have made the effort more recently."

It has paid off. Our conversation is conducted entirely in almost word-perfect English. I am again shamed at the lack of my Chinese.

"So in a year's time will Beijing have changed do you think?"

"Probably not too much in the building of new developments. I think it has really already been done, but I think the attitude of the people will have moved on again. Attitudes have changed here even in the past few years and

I believe that they will continue to change. People in Beijing are much more connected with the rest of the world. I really hope that more and more people will care more about the world and less about themselves. I hope that people will care less just about money and making money."

I ask him if he will think of returning to China since so many people leave and never return.

"The US is a developed country," he answers. "Although the weather in Beijing is not so good with the pollution, China is a developing country. In my industry I have read research that tells me that the opportunity in China is going to be immense in the future. The government has made more and more policies supporting the new energy vehicle sector. Certainly since 2004 there are more positive policies and more are coming which I know will encourage the industry further."

It is an interesting debate. The increased focus on new and alternative energy is a global issue and in a country the size of China, with the undoubted pollution issues, it is high on everyone's agenda. From central government moving high polluting industry away from the major cities to improve air quality, to the private individual buying face masks at the local store and monitoring air quality each day to see if their child should attend school, air pollution is a daily and much talked about hazard.

"BYD started in the new energy sector in China about the same time as Tesla (the US dual fuel car brand) did globally. The US policy is more mature than here in China. The Chinese automotive industry, and the new energy sector within it, is a big cake. Many people want to eat a slice of it. BYD is not a state-owned enterprise. It is basically a private one, so it is more difficult to develop the market than it would be if it were government owned. The critical thing is the access to charging points for the vehicles. In the US, there are many chargers but not in China. Here, there are very few. The infrastructure is young and underdeveloped. There are now more and more charging places in shopping mall car parks and Tesla have made big investments but more are needed. Everyone in the industry needs to invest so the opportunity for customers to really use the new energy vehicles, just as they are able to use any other, is equal. I believe it will happen. It is one of the big reasons I want to come back and to work in the industry. I can see the opportunity here."

We spend some time discussing the issues. It is clear that the future of new energy vehicles will be enormous in China, regardless of which company gets what share. At the heart of the development will be investment in infrastructure. It will need deep pockets. Zhong Shan and I agree that the most likely driver will be central government supporting the major State Owned Enterprises (SOE) in the electricity supply companies and major vehicle manufacturers.

The Chinese market in this area is as complicated as in any other but we agree that the will seems to be there on all sides. Brands that no one outside China will have heard of, assuming they have even heard of Tesla, are growing. The dual fuel 'Qin' (which BYD brought out to compete with the Tesla) took part in and won the first Formula Electric Grand Prix staged in Beijing in 2014. Reporters flocked to see it and many bemoaned the lack of atmosphere from the quiet revolution taking place before them as cars swept past at impressive, but soundless, speeds. "The Qin can reach a speed of 100kph in 5.9 seconds, alarmingly quietly" Zhong Shan enthuses. Technology problems such as battery life and charging times are being overcome and reaching broadly acceptable levels.

"The 'Tang' was also a new dual fuel car produced in 2005 and the 'Teng Shi' has been successfully launched as a joint venture between Daimler Benz and BYD at the end of 2014 in Beijing."

Zhong Shan has a real grip on the industry and his enthusiasm for it is genuinely infectious. It is no surprise to me that he was a successful regional sales manager. He is a convert and almost apostolic in his pitch patter.

"It is the smart choice you know. Did you know that the Qin sold more than 10,000 units in Shanghai last year?"

"I did not."

"The Qin is unfortunately not on the new energy-approved list in Beijing or I am sure it would be doing well here too."

I was unaware of such a list existing. I am always surprised by the complex web of local government regulations, rules, policies, subsidies and incentives across China.

"There is a central government subsidy available for the purchase of new energy cars," He explains.

"Is there?!"

"Yes. If you buy such a car in Shanghai, then you get a central government subsidy and you will also get a local government subsidy as cars like the Qin are on the local government new energy vehicle approved list. If you buy in Beijing, then you just get the national subsidy."

I don't bother to voice my thoughts about how the approved list might be compiled or agreed but it is clearly a critical list to be on across China if you are a manufacturer. I may have misheard him but I thought he told me that the subsidy could be as much as 50%. Now that is an incentive for greening China's congested city centres.

# The WeChat millionaire

Look up 'edutalent China' on any Western Internet browser and you will find lots of references to education and talent management but you may not find Sam Yang's business.

However, if you have the good fortune to be a WeChat user and can read Chinese, go to 'pdachina'. Specifically if you are a recent parent suffering the joys of bringing up an 'alien creature' with which you have never been taught to cope, you may find something interesting there. I would not normally promote the business of anyone I interview but I feel compelled to draw this small-but-perfectly-formed business to the attention of the world.

I was supposed to meet him at 09.00 but arrived a little early at 08.52, having spent an hour negotiating the Beijing commuter scrum on my way to the Western reaches of the city. We had hoped to meet in my eponymous coffee shop but a change in both our schedules meant I had to forego my early morning coffee and make the journey out to him.

Sam Yang is already at his desk, though he admits later that he was still in bed at 8am. There is a welcome smell of tea to greet me as well as the warmth and unusually firm handshake of 'Sam'. This is unusual, as most Chinese people do not go in for the bone-crushing American grip or even the polite-but-firm British clinch. But Sam Yang is no ordinary Chinese man.

At first, we struggle through the complexities of the English language since I do not have my trusty translator with me this time. It was all a bit last minute sorting the interview, what with Chinese New Year only 10 days away and many people already having left Beijing for their home towns and families. However, Sam finds the solution with 'Baidu translate', the Chinese equivalent (one ought to say better version) of Google Translate.

"I was born in AnKang in Shanxi province in 1970. I grew up in the country next to the famous Hanshui (Han River) in the shadow of Qinling (one of the most sacred and famous mountains in China). My only real memory of my childhood is hunger."

Not a bad opening remark to start our discussion. I am drawn in by the mystical images of a mist-shrouded mountain and a roaring mighty river next to which perches a small village populated only by farmers scraping a meagre living from the poor soil. However, as with all dreams of romanticism, the reality was much harder to bear.

"Life was very hard but we were happy," he says. "I was the eighth child of three older brothers and four older sisters. My eldest sister has a daughter who is the same age as me. It was normal in those days to have a big family. Especially as farmers. We struggled."

"I went back to my home village three years ago. Everyone had moved to the cities. There was almost no one left but the old and the very young. My school had many children when I was there but when I visited there were only 10 kids in the whole school. People want their children educated in the cities. It was very sad to see such a big change. I felt that I could have drawn some love and warmth from going back there, like I did when I was young. But I could not. There was almost no one there I knew. My feeling is that in another few years the whole village will have disappeared, perhaps a few people left."

There is a long reflective pause, punctuated by the pouring of more tea.

"I went to college in 1990 in Xi'an. I attended Shanxi Normal University and read biology. I did this at school so had no real choice about what I had to do at college. I was there for four years and then stayed in Xi'an for another year working as a computer engineer."

I look at him quizzically, biology then a computer engineer?

"I liked it."

"Ok."

"I then went back to school. I had worked a year and got enough money to afford to pay for the next three years. I went to the South West Normal University in Chongqing. I did what I had always wanted to do which was psychology. I didn't like biology. I did psychology because I really believed it would make me a better human being. I was actually rather unhappy at Xi'an university. I felt like I was inferior. I felt that I was the poorest student in the college as I had come from such a poor village and had no money at all. I enjoyed the three years studying psychology although I was a bit lonely studying this new subject. Then I came to Beijing."

I am still reeling from the openness and candid nature of his story. It was a bit brutal and it came almost faster than I could write, though the brief Baidu moments helped sort through the flow of consciousness.

"Why Beijing? It's a terribly expensive place without a job to come to isn't it?"

"I wanted to work here. It is everyone's dream to come to the big city from the farmlands. I was a country boy and this is the dream city. I lived in Tsinghua University, as it was the cheapest place I could find to stay and to eat. It was only ¥25 (£2.75) a night for the bed and I could eat in the university canteen for only ¥5 (55p) a day! I only had ¥300 (£33) in my pocket when I arrived in Beijing".

How on earth did you survive? Have you been here ever since?

"Yes. Of course I needed to get a job pretty quick but I had no idea how to get one. I didn't have a resumé, nothing. I didn't know where to go or what to do.

So I started walking around and talking to people to see if I could find a job."

And you found one before your money ran out? I am amazed at the sheer and total commitment of the man. He arrived without the means to go back. The ticket home would have burnt all his money and he would have gone back to nothing, with nothing. Perhaps that was the motivation to stay and make it work.

"Yes. I got a job... (Baidu translate to the rescue) as a .... (try again) .....in a warehouse. I started work for a computer company on ¥300 (£33) a month. It was not much but I was so happy that I was living in the dream city and had a job. The company had a dormitory for its workers so I had somewhere to sleep too and plenty of new friends at work. We worked together and played together. There were 10 of us in the dorm. I was very happy."

So you stayed there for a while?

"Oh no. After a year I started my own company."

Another surprise. His comment was as matter of fact as discussing the weather in the UK. So, after being without a Kuai to his name only a year earlier, and a year after working in a computer warehouse, Sam was setting up a company?

"Yes. It was a computer software and ..... (Baidu to the rescue) systems integration company. We had GE and Ericsson as our customers."

As I said at the start of this chapter, Sam Yang is no ordinary man. As we talk it becomes clear that his previous year had opened up a good many doors for him. He had managed to land his job with a computer repair company, which had already got the contract for repairing computers for GE and Ericsson in China, specifically in Beijing.

"They sent all their computers to us and they trusted us. We got to know the guys very well personally so myself and a few friends decided to set up our own business and take the customers with us. So we did."

I can't imagine how the old bosses felt when that sort of work walked out the door with 20 employees but I could guess.

"We developed the business slowly and carefully but after eight years we had a business that had sales of over ¥1.0bn. (£110 million) Then I quit."

What? I really could not take it in. Why would this obviously very successful entrepreneur just stop it all and start again. Perhaps serial entrepreneurs in the West know why, but I have to admit being somewhat in awe of Sam.

"Well, I was the general manager of Beijing and my friend was the general manager of Shanghai. We had really done well but I wanted to do something else. It was 2002 and I quit."

"To do what?"

"I had two years rest."

You had a 2-year rest?

"Well, I had enough money and I wanted time to think about what I wanted to do for the rest of my life."

It turns out that Sam also got married in 2002. They met though a friend. She has her own business and is clearly a successful business entrepreneur in her own right.

"I stayed in Beijing. I had made money but it was still in a relatively small company. I liked to do the work for GE and Ericsson but I had not really learned about their business model, how they managed cash flow, how they made money. I had been a general manager but I had never really learned, or been taught, how to manage. I decided I wanted to go to a big company but I realized I couldn't speak English and to work for an international company I needed English. I decided to learn English but I did not want to go to school again but to learn on the job if I could. I prepared a resumé and started looking. I was fortunate to get a job at Wall Street English as a 'cost consultant' or salesperson. I spent four years there and did every course they offered so I was able to learn English, while rising to become the deputy centre manager in the Guomao area of Beijing. I had 40 people working for me at the end."

He pauses.

"But you quit?" I am getting the hang of his pauses.

"Yes. In 2007, I quit and went to New Oriental (the largest provider of private education services in China). I spent two years there and became a centre director."

"Then you quit?" I chip in during another tea brew.

"Yes. How did you know?"

"Lucky guess."

"I went to Disney English as a ..."

"Centre director?"

"Yes."

"How long before you quit?"

"Two years."

"And..."

"I started my own company."

"This company?"

"Yes. I had spent 10 years learning about this type of business and I decided that I had learned enough to start my own business on my own. I had learned about managing cash flow, about business modelling, about how to manage people. It was 2011. It was the right time to do it."

"So it is now 2015. How has it been? How many employees do you have now?"

"It has been even better than I could have imagined. I am on my own. I worked out I don't need to employ anyone to run this business. I work about three days a week and spend the other four days with my young son. I believe I have finally achieved my dream of managing work and life together in the right balance. More importantly, I have a business which really helps people. Now I train fathers and mothers to be qualified parents."

"Interesting. How does that work?"

"I learned from Disney English. They had a programme aimed at parents with children between the ages of two and 12. During my time there, I was able to speak to and interview more than 6,000 families. I realized that people just don't prepare for their children. They encounter so many problems with their children. Suddenly there is a baby, in China it is their only one and their only chance to bring up a child. There is a big pressure on parents. Yet they are totally unprepared. They don't understand their child, they don't understand their husband, or their wife, how the baby will affect them and each other and their relationships."

As Sam outlines his business and the model that underpins it, I am captivated by its simplicity and strength. All good businesses meet a genuine need in consumers. In China, there is the perfect social and emotional storm to allow his business to prosper. A long-standing one-child policy that, despite being relaxed more recently, still leaves parents reticent about the costs associated with that second child. Add to this the enormous social pressure of marriage at a relatively young age for women, to have a baby quickly and for the grandparents to 'help' bring up the 'perfect' baby, ideally a son. The expectations are high but the expertise is low. There are no anti-natal or post-natal classes to attend, society frowns on those who 'can't cope' and there is little or no support for such conditions as post-natal depression. Against this backdrop: enter Sam.

"There is such a need among women," he continues. "But many in society don't realize they need training to be parents, it's true. But those people are not my target audience. In Beijing, GDP is rising. There is an emerging group of people who are waking up to the fact that they need to be better equipped to bring up their child. They have many problems. It is there that I see the chance for me to make money and to genuinely meet a need in society. Clearly it is not all parents that are going to be my customers. It is those parents who know they have problems and understand that they need help."

The market logic is compelling and the need clear but how on earth does he get customers? There are tens of millions of families within an hour of his small office in Haidian but how does he get to them?

"WeChat"

Sam has developed a brilliantly effective approach using a ubiquitous internet tool which is free to all in China. WeChat is as mentioned in previous chapters, a mixture of Facebook, Twitter, YouTube and eBay all in one, with a few extra bells and whistles including a direct payment system and short voice and video mail. All for free!

"I use WeChat to let people know about the courses I run and once people have been on them I encourage them to use WeChat to tell their friends and to engage with this business, me, as much as they like to get the support they need."

"How do you get customers then?"

"At first I thought I would have to use the same techniques as Wall Street English and the other providers that I worked for, using a call centre to use lists to get leads which I can then give free tasters to and then to sell the bigger more expensive courses to them. But no! I realized I didn't need to do that. WeChat allows me to get to customers with no costs at all. WeChat has changed my life!"

I am not sure if anyone can claim that Twitter or Facebook has actually changed their lives, though I know some who claim that eBay has. Nevertheless, it is a major claim and one I am sure WeChat would be pleased to hear!

"How?"

"It's simple: 80% of my customers come from WeChat. It is just me in my company so once I had set up this office, I just needed to get a few people on the first course. I had confidence that I had sufficient expertise and experience and qualifications to make a difference to parents so I know the product is a good one. I just needed and need people to try it and I was convinced it would take off from there. It has!"

Sam explains his business model. I feel sharing it is ok since I don't know anyone able to replicate it and indeed Sam is happy to share it with anyone who wants to take up his offer to be trained by him to become qualified as a parent coach and to set up their own business under his guidance. So, for ¥3,300 (£360) you attend a three-day course on parenting. That's it. If you want to, you can then take his four-day 'train the trainer' course for ¥12,800 (£1,400). That's it too. Simple. The trained trainers repeat the course after a year for free and they can teach with Sam as an assistant on his course once in the year if they wish, for nothing. There is another potential step which Sam has chosen not to take yet, where the trainers may pay Sam a small consideration for each person they in turn train. In his plan this seems a way off for now. In any event, his business model clearly works as he proudly shows me his bank account on WeChat, which after only three months has a rather healthy positive look about it!

"I am even making money while I sleep." He beams at me.

"I have used all my psychology training and all my years learning the business models of other businesses to get to where I am now. I know how to develop this business. I have even used the Disney English business plan model to do my calculations and I fully expect to be able to earn around ¥600,000 (£65,650) a month in the future. But this has taken 10 years of my life to develop the model specifically for this offering and me. I have also learned that I do not need to manage people. It is a waste of time. I don't need to. I can outsource everything I need help with, from finance to marketing. I want to put all my time into researching and applying the psychology of parenting so I can help people be better parents."

The numbers are nothing short of astonishing. It is a simple model, with a simple proposition, meeting a clearly untapped market need in the growing market of increasingly empowered women and wealthier middle classes of Beijing, and in time, further afield no doubt.

"I have six volunteers who work for me for free," he explains. "These women feel that the course has helped them so much. They have seen material improvements in their relationships with their child as well as their husband. So they want to help me spread this knowledge and the course to as many parents as possible."

There is also something deeper we discuss.

"Many women have been hurt through their relationships with their husbands. This is a big problem in China. They have suffered and felt terrible personal pain. They tell me that the course has helped them feel warm in their hearts as a result. Over 50% of my students are referrals from those who have already attended my course and 90% are women, though I do get some fathers too. Women have such pressure on them in China. I want to give people hope and help them to feel positive about themselves."

This is clearly a significant untapped need in China. Does he think he can go further to help women deal with these pressures?

"No. I am really not qualified to do that. I know the limits of my course and I will not go further into psychological consulting. That is not my area and not the business opportunity for me. I don't have the competences to do that."

Has he applied the course to his own life?

"I think I am a good father. My wife tells me that since I started doing this work she has seen a very positive change in me."

"Has she been on the course?"

"No! She runs her own business and is busy with that all the time and travelling on business. She doesn't want to do the course to be taught by me. I try my best to be a good father. Every night I read two stories to my son. He is still young. I play with my son, I do everything with my son. Being with my son is good for him, to have his father around, for his development. I work and teach for three days each week and the other four days I play with my son. Money is not so important to me now. I have enough money."

So how does he feel after all these years and doing what he is doing now?

"I believe that if you do valuable things for people then the money will come. I truly believe this and so far I have been right. I really enjoy my job. I think that I will be able to help many women, many children and some husbands."

He smiles at me. It is a smile of a man who does what he loves, has found the peace and place that he craved from the early 'inferior' university years. We share a final cup of tea.

"I am living my dream. Many people in China can't."

He is right, and he is lucky, self-made lucky.

# The Chinese-American

She looks like any other professional Chinese woman as she bustles through the door. Joyce Chao orders her latte in flawless Mandarin, her strong Asian features fooling the serving staff as much as they do pretty well everyone else in the place apart from me, but then I know her. Once she has sat down I have her usual friendly greeting, in flawless English.

"You eaten yet?"

It's mid-afternoon but it's a common Chinese greeting. Food is important and the lack of it has been a Chinese curse for centuries. It's why you really never see rice left in a bowl at meal times. The greeting also defines the underlying politeness and thoughtfulness, which permeates all relationships here, personal and professional. She visibly relaxes when I smile and nod.

Sipping her latte Joyce looks every bit the businesswoman she is, but there is a critical difference from the others bent over work papers around us. Joyce is Chinese-American.

"It doesn't matter where I grew up, or what colour my passport is, because I look Chinese," she says. "I have Chinese blood and heritage. Being Chinese is in my core. I jokingly tell my friends I am now half Beijinger since I've been here for 12 years. However, the Chinese in me comes out with an American touch and delivery. It can be a bit direct and to the point sometimes but this is why I feel I can add value. My mainly US clients want clarity and certainty. In a culture where communication is more subtle and passive, I provide a balance and that's where I hope I offer value and why I get paid."

Joyce is second generation Chinese from the US. She grew up there with American schooling and a rich corporate work experience. In 2003, a keen interest in learning more about her own Chinese culture and language prompted her to respond to an education management job advertisement based in Beijing. She got it, moved and has been here ever since.

She's had to adjust and adapt over the years in Beijing but she's retained her US openness and candour. She has a big heart and a warm, effervescent and endearing personality. Since arriving in Beijing more than a decade ago, she has managed to combine her personal style of fast talking and passionate delivery with a deep attention to the details of the cultural differences and idiosyncrasies of 'the Chinese way'. The result is a dual language and dual culture expert advisor.

Having worked with a variety of UK and US businesses operating in China, Joyce has a very well developed sense of what works and what doesn't. She's seen all shapes and sizes of business try and succeed, as well as fail, in their efforts to enter China and/or position themselves here.

"In such a fast-developing economy with many changes and challenges I can't say there is a definitively right way of doing things here but there are certainly wrong ways. Time and again I see advice and good intentions fall by the wayside. The negative impact is not often immediate but time will tell. My role as an advisor is to offer ideas and solutions, and I don't hold back informing clients of the risks. However, at the end of the day, the decisions of how to do business in China belong to the client. The core of any strategy and advice that I offer is to aim to build up the relationship base and not to do anything that might tear it down."

"Doesn't it frustrate you when you see things happen that you have tried to guard against?" I ask.

"Sure it does. But I am older and wiser now. I've come to understand the simple fact that China's big, with a long history of over 5,000 years. Yes, there are other civilizations with many years of history, but none so colourful and fragmented in the past 60 years as China's. Certainly nothing comparable to the past decade of miraculous transformation here. The frustration is not always an 'I told you so.' It's that modern China is a big but constantly moving target. What I experienced in 1987, my first trip to Beijing, is vastly different from what my best friend's first trip was like in 2007. And it's just the amazing ways and speed of things. I'd like to say it is bewilderment more than frustration."

"Like what?"

"There was one business trip when I was only away a week and they totally renovated the Laitai flower market! It was astonishing! I'm quite cautious in advertising what I do. I make mistakes and learn from them. They help me minimize the unknowns and allow me to manage the constant changes and cultural faux pas we non-Chinese all make."

Joyce is a bundle of energy as we talk. She's constantly multi-tasking on her smartphone, email and of course, the ubiquitous WeChat. She seems to know everyone and everyone knows Joyce. She is a 'do it now' person, arranging connections, making meetings. She works quickly, knowing that in China if you don't seize the moment, it's gone.

"You know, I have been so fortunate. My parents' generation experienced a revolution which was gritty and horrid but in the past 12 years I've had the privilege of experiencing a different revolution in China – one of technology and economics. It's humbling and it's what drives me. My parents' and grandparents' generations paved the way for me to do what I can do in China."

"So what do you actually do?"

"Coming to China mid-career and possessing a developed knowledge of both sides of the ocean, I suppose you could best describe me as a cultural guide and, at times, 'fixer'. It's my business to use my sort of chameleon role to know how to get things done in building the international bridge in China. I've many Chinese friends from all over the world whom I've helped and who can help me when I call on them. Relationships are important anywhere in the world but they are vital here. It's not a chore to keep up with these either. These people are my friends as well as good long-standing acquaintances. I enjoy spending time with them and we all help each other whenever we can. That's how it is here. That's what relationships (Guangxi) are all about."

As a Chinese-American does that have an effect on how people see you?

"If I don't open my mouth no one can tell the difference," Joyce says with a wink.

"I've opinions and solutions that I have to hold back at times. It's not what the Chinese are used to, not from a woman, and one who looks Chinese. But people are very accommodating and gracious. They'll hear me out, because I'm a foreigner, but I'm caught in the middle sometimes. People here expect me to understand the Chinese approach of decision-making and my overseas clients want results. At times the locals default to 'you don't understand what we mean because you didn't grow up here'…"

She shrugs her shoulders with a feigned look of confusion. Her phone vibrates continuously and she flips out a few more WeChats as we pause.

"Because I've always been involved in education and in writing as a profession I'm often asked to write or review English speeches or materials for some of my Chinese contacts. There's never any talk of money or getting paid for such 'favours'. It's part of relationship building and people tend to understand it's part of the 'favour bank' between friends and friends of friends. The Chinese have an amazing ability to weigh up and balance the right level of reciprocal favours between each other. When I explain this to clients they often balk at the expectation that they are to do something for nothing. Many simply refuse. That's when the trouble starts. Remember what I said about relationships earlier?"

How could I forget? Joyce delivers her messages so you don't forget them easily.

"Back home in the West, we often help friends move, offer them lifts in our cars and the like. We don't expect payment. So what's the big deal? Is it because some businesses really see China more as a client, than as a friend?"

Ignoring the deeper philosophical or socio-political point for a moment she nevertheless leaves a pause long enough for it to sink in before she continues.

"I try to help whenever I can. The rule is 'don't promise something you can't deliver'. Sometimes you just have to help. It's the right thing to do because even though there are many shiny high-rise buildings all over the cities of China, it's still a developing country. Among other things it's still trying to catch up from the lost generation resulting from the Cultural Revolution. Occasionally you feel you are being taken for granted but that's a very Western perspective. From the Chinese side they will not see it like that and would be very offended if they thought you believed it."

Where Joyce seems to excel is in the highly ambiguous area of 'reading between the lines' of meaning, actions and words of the Chinese.

On a related note I believe that there's a remarkable similarity between the British and the Chinese. There used to be a joke about the so called 'Whitehall Mandarins' of British government never being clear about what they meant. For those who have ever seen the old British TV series Yes Minister or Yes Prime Minister, this will make a good deal of sense. The British are often known for being opaque and for the use of euphemisms. The Chinese excel in this art. Reading between the lines of what is said to understand what is actually meant requires a very good cultural translator as well as linguistic interpreter. Joyce is both.

"Something different, and what might be hard for Westerners to understand is that Chinese, both as a language and as a culture, is all about context, symbols and layers of meaning. We love lucky numbers: seven and eight. And nine means longevity. Also just don't think about using the number four in lifts, signage, seating, anything. In Chinese, four is too close to the character for death. References to historical characters, old sayings and proverbs as well as odd plays on words and even Chinese characters or political figures really helps the Chinese understand the deeper meaning of the comment. To them, it is second nature. Even to me, and certainly to my clients, it can seem unfathomable and the subject of significant confusion."

So how to survive this complexity?

"Basically accept it. And get a good Chinese strategist, one that has the perspective and modern history knowledge. It's the fact for all cultures; outsiders will never be able to make full sense of it. Having someone around to help keep you straight, and away from the cultural landmines, is always useful."

She smiles at me knowingly.

"I should add what I've been seeing more and more of. International businesses and organizations go out and recruit for China without asking a few additional questions of applicants. They probably don't appreciate that the Chinese have a set of very specific views on other cultures. They've not been exposed to the multicultural and cosmopolitan cities of the West or the complexity of businesses that cross borders. It's a mistake for Western businesses here to employ people just because they look or sound Chinese. It might seem silly but I still see global brands employing Cantonese speakers from Hong Kong or South East Asia. Unfortunately, mainland Chinese don't see Hong Kong as the vibrant global city we do. There's deep suspicion of Hong Kongers, not to mention that Cantonese might sound the same to the untutored ear but it's not the same language as 'Putonghua', the mainland language."

Joyce will not discuss the other prejudices against the Japanese, Singaporeans, and regrettably, minorities within China. However, a brief look at Chinese history will educate you to the long-standing mistrust and concerns that plague current Chinese thinking. 'The rape of Nanjing' and the long Sino-Chinese war, as well as the opium wars and other struggles with everyone from the British to the Dutch, are worth being aware of.

"Something else here that always confuses clients is the total lack of diaries," adds Joyce.

A change in topic is probably called for, I've mentioned this elsewhere. But Joyce elaborates.

"It's CFD."

What?

"CFD, Chinese Fire Drill. Everything seems to be last minute, fast and furious, well-managed but all in a massive hurry. That's why you have to seize the moment and do everything straight away. The whole place, most businesses and pretty well everyone's private life is managed on an 'are you in Beijing?, are you free tonight, tomorrow, the day after?' basis. Trying to arrange schedules for overseas visitors who expect everything mapped out in advance and set in an organized diary is a nightmare. It's a very big education process for Westerners. No matter how many times I tell them they still don't believe it. Even the VIPs may not have a diary. They have to keep time somehow but in China they simply can't plan much time in advance."

Doesn't this make it all a little difficult to do things even booking flights and hotels?

"Hotels are easy, there's so much spare capacity here, getting a room is never a problem. The flights are also often all booked at the last moment, except for some of the international ones, which usually need a bit of forward planning. However, after that it's a free for all. Within very strict Chinese guidelines of course. If you're senior you will get a meeting with most people, if you're not then don't count on getting a meeting at all, certainly not above your own level of seniority, unless you are accompanying someone more senior. This goes right to the top and the hierarchy of who should be seen and for how long and where is played out at intergovernmental as well as corporate level."

I have personally got used to arriving in China after a break or business trip with no diary plan at all from one week to the next. I know that after a few WeChats or emails my diary will fill with the people I need to see and those who want to see me. It's a bizarre experience at first but after a while you get used to it. Helping colleagues cope is another matter and here the degree of trust required is very high. Many people arriving for the first time, or even after a few visits, fail to appreciate the complexity of the Chinese way of working, particularly the total lack of diaries. Such is the culture shock to many arriving in China I find myself usually engrossed in an hour or so of pre-briefing to colleagues. The level of incredulity at some of my explanations and what to expect is invariably high. Fortunately, we know each other well enough for them to listen hard to the briefings and work together to get the best result from their visits.

"I've known really senior guys arrive at the airport not knowing which hotel they are staying at, who will be picking them up, whether they have a dinner to go to straight away or what the agenda is for the next day. I mean they do have a general idea and with a few end goals but never the specifics. These are the best people at getting things done in China. They are the old hands (with a high level of tolerance for the unknown) who know that by the time the aircraft gets to the gate they will be met, greeted, transported, fed and watered in the right way and with the right people. It can go wrong sometimes, but equally the Chinese will pull out all the stops to ensure the senior visitor as well as the local leader does not lose 'face'.

"It can be incredibly frustrating and you can't always be certain of the seniority of everyone round the meeting or dinner table. But people can mobilize very quickly and I've known flights changed and schedules dropped and or rescheduled, even using double bookings and two dinners to attend in an evening being arranged so that the right 'face' can be shown and the right people met and spoken too. It really is almost an art form of organizational logistics. It's quite impressive!"

Joyce is in her element now. This is her life and she makes her living fron. managing the complexity and ambiguity of Chinese etiquette and hierarchical management, all in the interests of getting things done and continuing to build that international bridge.

So with so many Chinese people studying overseas and English levels increasing, is there still a role for your type of service? The cultural bridge and interpreter?

"Definitely yes – and even more so. People like me – fortuitously alive at such a time as this – we come with experience, insights and perspective. Many only see a part of the culture they enter. Chinese students only get the academic experience plus some work time. They might know US or British culture as a consumer but do they really know enough about what Americans or British people think? On the other hand, foreigners come to China, learn the language and love the cuisine, but do they have Chinese friends from all walks of life and know enough about how the Chinese think? A more key question is do they care enough to try to know?

"While I say this, I also know that advisors with my background have a limited window. It's a matter of time. The Chinese have passed the stage where they were the hungry recipients of international business thinking. In any event, most senior leaders here are well-travelled, speak almost perfect English and have read more management books than you have. Many have overseas degrees and overseas expertise is a lot easier to obtain. They don't need advice much longer. They are now the consumers as well as the business owners of the emerging global market. Goods and services might be created elsewhere in the world but they are now sold, usually through joint venture partnerships, to the millions of Chinese who have cash now. It's moved from 'made in' to 'sold in' China."

This is a recurring theme in almost every discussion I've ever had here personally. Business can succeed in China but not by applying the old models. People like Joyce can provide the support necessary to avoid the cultural traps but businesses now need to arrive in China with quite a different mindset from a few years ago.

"There remains so much opportunity here. From education and healthcare, specifically care of older people, to handmade chocolates and high-street fashion. The top end gift market, from wines to handbags and watches, has been hit by the anti-graft purge of the government and everyone actually applauds that initiative. However, there remains so much that can be done, and to go for, in specialty markets and many others too!"

Joyce should know. It's where she works and is very successful.

# "the fruit man

The telephone line to North East Australia is poor. It is a bad line.

Actually, it is not supposed to be like this. I had arranged the interview some time ago but we had not managed to meet before Chinese New Year and Lu Pin Shen's departure on a cruise with his parents around New Zealand and Australia for the Chinese New Year intervened on my somewhat tight editor schedule.

"They may never get the chance to go again so I wanted to really make this a special trip," he had told me.

So here we are. Me ensconced in my seat against the wall in the coffee shop and Lu Pin Shen (or Sing as he prefers to be known) in a hotel bedroom somewhere not far from Cairns in Australia. We both have free Internet so we decide we can use the free phone facility provided by WeChat. I suppose we could use the free video link system but the phone seems to be the best option for intermittent and low-strength internet signals, at both ends. An amazing piece of technology and so simple to use.

"How is the weather there?"

I tell him not to be too smug, he knows full well that Beijing is freezing at this time of the year. Clearly Cairns is not.

Sing is technically a Hong Kong resident although he was born in Xi'an in 1968; his mother is from Sichuan and his father Shanghai. They are both

retired now but were among the early trade investors in Hong Kong and clearly didn't do too badly. Despite all this, Sing lives in Beijing, where he has a house, when he has time to visit the city.

"I was lucky enough to be able to study in the US. I went to Vanderbilt University in Tennessee then moved back and worked for my parents for a bit. However, in 2000 I set up a hi-tech company in the US, which did ok. I ran that until 2005/6 and then sold it. I didn't make a lot of money but it was a good experience and I made a bit. I started to look for opportunities back in China and by pure chance I got into raspberries."

"You did what?"

"Raspberries. I know, it does sound a bit strange".

"Yes."

I'd thought it was a bad line but Sing is deadly serious.

"Most of my friends were into hi-tech or were in finance. I know from my own experiences that Hi-tech is all about all or nothing. You either do really well and you make money or you lose it. I realized that no one was in to agriculture. I became fascinated by it as a business opportunity after a while. If you spend money in agriculture, unlike hi-tech, you won't lose everything even if the weather is bad. China has 1.3 billion people and there is a fundamental foundation in agriculture. It just needs to be modernized."

Sing is right. Even though there is an inexorable shift from the rural economy to the increased urbanization of China, it still needs to feed itself. The agricultural system remains largely archaic in many provinces and rural areas, despite the significant reforms, which have taken place over the past 30 years. It is still dogged mainly by family plots serving themselves or local markets. Highly commercialized farming does take place, of course, but there is significant room for improvement.

"The need is there but not a lot of money is put into agriculture. I realized that it is not quite as easy as I thought, but it's not an impossible task. There's a lot of potential. You are dealing with a very broad cross section of people including some of the poorest in society. Also, believe me, dealing with local village officials is not easy. The internet is a lot easier to deal with than soil and plants and farmers but I decided to get into raspberries as an entry point in agriculture. People in China don't know what raspberries are. They are a really new fruit here. Given all my experience over the past few years, and I've had a few failures, I am the raspberry expert now."

Soft fruit is sold all over China as in any country but the common strawberry, for example, was only introduced to China in the late 1980s, according to Sing, and blueberries didn't make an appearance until 2000.

"You just don't see raspberries at all. One primary reason is there is limited know-how as it is a complicated fruit to grow to a high quality and high yield. In the UK, the fruit is common but not in China. I believe that in the next five to 10 years, the raspberry will be as common and as successful as the strawberry and blueberry have been. I want to be the one that does that!"

Sing has a very clear perspective on his primary target group, both from a demographic as well as a geographic perspective. His target audience is the health conscious middle classes of China. Specifically, he sees his first target as the sprawling metropolis of Shanghai.

"Maybe 5% of the Chinese population know about raspberries, possibly even less. However, foreigners know about them and they are familiar with them so I know that's a ready market. Also, Chinese people who have been abroad will also be aware of the raspberry. There is a market there. Of course, the biggest market is the ordinary citizen. I have been working with resellers and wholesales. These guys are always looking for new fruit. Many have tried raspberries but failed as the varieties that have been available have been low quality and low yield."

Sing and I discuss what I find to be a fascinating marketing problem. Since the traditional raspberry growing season is very short, only three months, it is in the public awareness for a short while and then disappears again so each year this presents the wholesalers and the sellers with a struggle to reintroduce and re-launch this strange fruit anew. Needless to say, many have just given up. Sing has an interesting solution to this constant need for reintroduction.

"Do it once."

I'm convinced I lost him on the line. "Do what?"

"Do it once. Launch them then just keep producing them 24/7 and 365 days a year."

After a number of experimental, and I sensed, quite expensive, false starts over the past eight years, Sing has now identified the solution to the supply and awareness problem for this humble red super fruit. Greenhouses!

"The biggest problem has been the consistency of the quality of the fruit. There is a huge health conscious marketplace out there among the emerging middle classes of China. These people are worried about their, often only, child. They want the best for them and fruit is a big thing on their agenda. But it has to be fresh and good quality, ideally organically grown. The raspberry needs proper growing conditions, just enough water and just enough sun. I have approached the whole thing from a scientific point of view. I've applied the tools and techniques I learned in the hi-tech environment to raspberries. The main thing you need is to try to control the environment. Greenhouses help you do that."

"A friend of mine in the UK who is a grower told me something I think is funny. He said raspberries are like women. They are special, they need a lot of effort putting into them and if you put the effort in then they will repay it and you will be treated well. But if you don't put the right amount of effort in then you will have big trouble."

Sing chortles down the phone at me. I remain studiously and respectfully silent.

He tells me that he has been trying to grow raspberries in a few different places since 2006. He started in Hunan province in the middle of China to the South of the Xiang River but was not successful.

"Unfortunately it was just too far away from anywhere. The suppliers were not there and though labour was cheap, pretty well everything else from the foam boxes to the packaging had to be shipped in at great expense. Transportation costs were just one of a series of small individual problems that eventually made him give it up and move back into China.

"I have learned my lessons from my previous experimenting. We have now found the perfect place in Yinchuang city, Xinjin county in Ningxia province. It's in the West of China but it has a dry climate, transport links are excellent and I have located a very good site with excellent access to the airport. The sun is bright and the air is clear. It has a really good climate. With the greenhouses overcoming the problems of the wind in the area we can have a year round growing season. I know the sun can be strong there but by using the greenhouses efficiently we can pretty well control most of the adverse aspects of the weather and take full advantage of the good clean air and great soil. With the greenhouses you can eliminate the unknown elements like the wind and the rain."

This part of China is not unfamiliar with growing small red fruit. It is the centre of the goji berry production in China. The goji, sometimes known as the wolf-berry, is renowned in China for its medicinal properties. So the area certainly has the pedigree from that perspective. Sing also tells me that it is the centre of an increasing amount of Chinese wine production with French, Australian and German growers planting vines here.

Sing tells me he is returning to China after his long holiday with his parents to start building the greenhouses.

"What is the size of the facility you are building?"

"We will build in stages. The first stage is aiming at around 500kg a day. Once we get the quality right at that level then we will shift the production up to 5,000kg a day."

Sing delivers the numbers in such a neutral and straightforward manner that at first I miss the sheer size of production he is envisioning.

"We know from our planning that the Shanghai market alone can support around 500kg a day through the wholesalers and markets we have researched there. We will be investing around ¥20.0m (£2.16m) to set everything up and get started. From a distributor perspective I know a lot of people who have done strawberries and been successful. They have tried raspberries, liked them, but haven't managed to get it right on the quality and supply side. They are willing to give us a try. There are others who are still doing lower-quality raspberries and making money, so we know they will be interested once we can prove the quality side."

Sing expects to employ around 100 people at the facility to start with, including management, administration, farming and picking.

"Everyone will be full time from the very start. That is unusual in the soft fruit market, which has been seasonal. Until I arrived. The problem is that the pickers are seasonal migrants so I have to compete with the other producers of berries, wine and the like. We will have to fight for the labour. But we have a distinct advantage over everyone else."

Sing explains that most pickers work for three months, learn how to pick properly to a high quality, non-squashed, standard and then leave after the season's crop is finished. The next year the growers have to retrain people all over again so quality never really improves from one year to the next. Sing's strategy of offering full-time, year-round employment means that he can train the pickers and then retain them to pick at the high quality he needs to penetrate the market. It is a simple, and hopefully a competitive, strategy, which should make him money and keep it rolling in around the year. Solid long-term employment will be attractive as well; though he may lose the migrants, he should, he hopes, attract local pickers.

"We will be able to afford even to train people for six months, as long as they stay. Labour costs are increasing in China, but for this type of labour it is at least 10 times cheaper than in Australia and about seven times cheaper than the US, even though they are using migrant Mexican labour."

"What about the supply side?" I ask.

"Well, what I learned in Hunan comes in here. It was a lot more unstructured than where we are now. Locally, In Yinchuang city I can source everything I need. From packaging, the foam boxes, to soil care, glass and repair materials, everything. I have been very careful about everything. Location has been critical and the soil type and composition has been essential. I have paid a good deal of money to get the right research done and the right agricultural advice. I know this scientific approach will pay me back. I have tried to apply all I learned in the hi-tech world to this seemingly low-tech agricultural production facility. However, it is anything but low-tech. To get the right outputs I have put a lot into the right inputs."

Sing has gone to extraordinary lengths to employ the right people too. He has a German facility manager who lives locally.

"He is very precise in his approach. I need that type of almost scientific approach and precision of attitude to make this a success. I know he will be able to overcome many of the problems of growing raspberries in China."

Do you worry about competitors setting up and stealing your ideas and market share?

"It is very difficult for someone to do. On the surface, what we are doing looks simple. It would be a big mistake to think that though. This is a scientific and hi-tech approach, so it would be very difficult to copy. It is also very expensive to set up properly so I think we have a head start on our competitors which they will struggle to match or catch."

Sing expects to be in production soon, by the next growing season.

"We will be aiming for the best quality produce year round. This will allow us to be on the shelves all the time, not just for three months and then gone. We expect to be able to build distribution and market share as well as sustainable long-term brand awareness simply by being there when others are not!"

"What brand are you using, a Chinese or international one?"

"Actually, we don't have one at the moment but I hope to have a Chinese name alongside an international one so we can get the best of both worlds! The positioning is very important as we specifically want to target the middle classes with an eye to their, or their families', health."

"Will you just be Mr Raspberry or do you have ambitions for more than just raspberries?"

"I think this is a process. I believe that raspberries are a good entry point. If they are successful I may move into strawberries, blueberries, all at the top end of the quality spectrum. Also there is significant opportunity from moving into related products such as yogurts, flavoured milk, ice cream and other areas."

Sing is clearly passionate about his business and about the scientific approach he is taking.

"It's not just about the money. It's about doing this right and leaving a legacy. The variety type is critical and I have spent a long time and got a lot of advice on that. I really want to do it right."

Sing expects to be in production soon. If you are reading this and you are in China, look out for the raspberries. There is a pretty good chance if you find good ones they'll be Sing's!

# Facing West

Wrapped up in her almost ankle-length padded coat, Mrs Tara Li huddles into her seat. The winter wind is in the wrong direction and the only seats we can get are by the door. It keeps blowing open. Other customers and our erstwhile patron seem oblivious to our plight, so after a few pitiful efforts of ineffectual complaining we are forced to huddle into our corner and hope that the conversation will warm us up.

Tara was born in 1969 in Beijing and has never moved. She is a product of 'the movement' as she was at Peking University in 1989, the year of Tiananmen Square.

"That was in my second year at Peking University. I was reading psychology. I wasn't involved."

Everyone I meet who was in Beijing at that time tells me the same thing, either way.

"It really affected my job prospects when I left. No institutions would take students from Peking University at that time. It was difficult to get a job. Also, psychology was a new and unusual degree and people were suspicious. They didn't know what to do with me. I had hoped to go into a hospital job but they gave my job to a disabled person. They said they needed to balance the workforce."

She looks directly at me as she speaks and I feel this is a time to adopt the Chinese approach and read between the lines. The reader must do so too, as I would like my Visa renewed.

"I had no job. In those days, graduates were allocated jobs by the government. You went where you were allocated. If they said you had to be a secretary, then you went to be a secretary, no matter how good a degree you had. At that time the authorities looked at your university, your degree, your record, your family, everything. Then they decided where you'd work. Also 65% of your salary would go back to the company for 'costs' and you were left with the rest to live on. The university threatened to send me to a middle school to be the Communist Youth League leader. Can you imagine?! Me?! Do that job?! I said 'no'! They didn't like it."

Again she looks directly at me. Impassive features leaving me to draw my own conclusions.

"I see."

"I had relatives in the US, my mother's sister. They saw an advert for a French Company who produced interior decoration materials, curtains and the like, who wanted people in Beijing. I applied."

So, it took an advert in the US, for a French company, looking for someone in China, for Tara to get a job almost round the corner from where she lived?

"Yes. I got the chance to go for the interview. I was up against people with doctorates and sales management degrees. The French guy asked me what I could do. I said I'd just graduated from the best university in China. I was not the best but I was a good student. If I had got in through the hard entrance exams and then graduated I felt I could learn very fast and do well at whatever they gave me."

She laughs at the sheer audacity of it, the arrogance of youth.

"He gave me a chance. It was very poor pay but the manager of the showroom was leaving soon and she liked me so she taught me everything I needed to know about how to sell the products. I had to remember a lot. But I'd been a good student so it was ok. Many of the managers at the French company were foreigners so I was really lucky to get the job."

"Could you speak French?"

"Of course not! But I spoke English and of course I am Chinese so I knew how to use Chinese psychology."

That direct look again. More between the lines? I get confused sometimes.

"After my three months' probation I got a contract as a sales manager. The job wasn't the greatest challenge for me although I made many friends. In 1993, after a couple of years at it, I quit."

If the reader has dipped into a few of these Notes already, this will be a familiar comment from many people.

"Why?"

"Really it was down to my family. My mother thought I'd become a stranger to them. In those days a senior professor at a school would have earned ¥200/month (£20.16). I was earning five times that much and I was getting commission on top of that. I didn't have time to spend the money. Also, I really didn't know how much money I was earning. But I was working very hard. I got up very early and with entertaining clients in the evenings I would often not be home until 23.00. My family never saw me."

"It must have been tough for both of you."

"My mother said I was more like a Westerner than Chinese. I wore a smart suit every day and smart shoes. Not good. I was under a lot of pressure. Also, in my heart, I felt I had lost touch with my friends and with myself, so I decided to leave. I felt I was so busy making money from morning to night I couldn't reconcile my outer and my inner self."

She pauses for a long time, clearly reliving those feelings.

"I was lost."

So?

"I quit and stayed at home for three months and read books. Then my mother said, 'get a normal job'. Friends introduced me to a national, state-owned, company and I got a job as a secretary. My mother was happy that I'd got a suitable 'woman's job'."

Were you?

"I was not a good typist! At lunch time I would go out and spend money. My colleagues thought I was strange. I was only earning ¥400 (£40.34) a month but I was spending ten times that much. I tried to change a lot but it was so boring!"

"So what did you do? Quit again?"

"I tried to quit. I went to the department head but he said perhaps I could do a different job. The company was in the scientific instrument business. Import and export. They were setting up a new department to deal with exporting. They realized I could do something else and they said that they were patient enough for me to learn and to try this different job. So I said I would do the job but they had to give me the chance to choose my team and the products myself!"

The direct look again, but this time a self-conscious smile flickers across her face as she recalls the attitude of determination and confidence of her youth. It hasn't seemed to dissipate much over the years, from my perspective.

"There weren't many competitors and a few senior advisors helped us find some really good products. We sold measuring devices, scientific instruments and the like, with customers in the power industry as well as tobacco companies and others which needed accurate measures for their processes. We sold online and were very successful. However, I was under more and more stress again. There were no real policies to work to. We were governed by the ideas from the big boss."

This is an all too familiar story to me from across China. Hierarchies are everything in Chinese companies. Friends joke that in some businesses, the CEO decides the colour of the toilet rolls. Actually, I have never seen any colour other than white, but I get what they mean. Certainly corporate structures are nothing like the layered and delegated authorities of the classic Western business. In China, there are two types of people in a company: the workers and the bosses. The leaders decide everything, and the workers do as they are directed. Within some layers of authority there is scope for independent thought, but outside the strict boundaries the direction is top-down. It is changing, but slowly.

"We were also earning too much money!"

"In whose opinion?"

"That's what the finance department felt. In the beginning, the company took 70% of the revenues and we got 30% to split between us. But after the first year they told us that we were only going to get 10%. At first we thought this was terrible but we did the maths on the projections and realized we were still going to make a lot of money so we said ok. We had a real boom in contracts and were again accused of making too much money. Finance then said they were going to allocate all the costs of the business to us and we were not to be rewarded on revenue but net profit. At the end of the year, we had a huge quarrel with finance. They'd added in so many extra costs and would not tell us what many of them were. Also, in 1996, there were many more competitors who had entered the market, overseas companies and many within China. There were more resellers and more high pressure on us to compete."

Tara is retelling the history of China's late 1990s manufacturing boom. Her words reflect the realities of living through a time of China's 'opening up' to international competition. When 'Made in China' really took off. Her business felt this acutely.

"It became harder and harder to find products and to compete. Also, our competitors were not as 'clean' as us."

The direct look. I know what she means.

"As a state-owned enterprise we couldn't compete on 'financial support' to deals. I found it just too difficult to sell our products and to solve everything myself. It was then that I attended an exhibition to sell our products. It was quiet and I took the chance to walk around the other exhibitors.

"I stumbled on a stand from the Seattle MBA programme. The next day, I applied and in the week of the exhibition I attended the entrance exam. My score was not good as I was not so good at written English. The Dean gave me a chance, though, so I became one of the first group of MBA students at Seattle University in Beijing. It was really interesting as they flew in US professors every two months to lecture. I was working at the same time. It was tough doing a part-time course and many nights I just stayed in the office all night as the internet links were better there. I didn't sleep, just worked during the day and studied at night."

This amazing commitment to self-improvement is a characteristic of the Chinese that runs deep into history and is an ethic which many Westerns would do well to note and learn from, in my personal opinion.

"The learning was very different to the Chinese way. We could, and were expected to, challenge the professors. That's not the way in China. I became even more Western and influenced by Western thinking and approaches. My classmates were CEOs and high-level people from business. It was a stimulating and excellent experience. It was what I really wanted to do."

"So how did that affect your work and your career?"

"It was also then that I reviewed my heart to really think about how I felt and what I wanted to do and how to use my knowledge, my work experience and my feelings. I knew a little of human resources and decided this could combine with my psychology degree as well. I decided to tell my boss that I wanted a change. He said ok!"

"How did you know where to start, what to do, how to make a difference?"

"It wasn't easy to start with, mainly as HR was under the control of the government and I had to operate according to government rules and approaches. I couldn't use the theory I'd just learned. The government forbade it! So I quit."

A recurring theme here.

"Where did you go?"

"I went to work for Legend Computers, the forerunner of Lenovo. I was called up by a head hunter who said they wanted someone who had a psychology degree and HR experience. The job seemed made for me. Unfortunately, as a government worker, I had an apartment with my job and I lost that when I left. It was a really big decision to move. Also, in those days, it was a very strange company, at least in my eyes. I had to get involved with performance appraisals and assessing all the managers, from scratch. I managed to get it all done inside six months but then I really had had enough by then. The company was just too stretched and strange  It had 42 leaders. Before every meeting everyone had to stand and sing the company song and repeat the names of the founders. It was like a cult. I didn't like it. It seemed like the old days in China when everyone had to recite the mantra of allegiance to Chairman Mao. They said they wanted to promote me but since I was 'having problems', I was visibly not participating in the singing, they wanted me to sit a 'cultural exam'. I didn't. So I left."

"To go where?"

"I joined a joint venture company between Legend and a software business. I also had to move locations as Legend was in the north west of Beijing but the new company was in the centre, so I moved and bought an apartment for my parents. But it just wasn't to be. After two years the government changed the rules and the business folded and I was out."

Tara moved to a Hong Kong business selling fashion-wear. The HQ was in Hong Kong and she joined at a time when they were opening new stores. She managed the opening of 42 stores across Beijing alone, responsible for HR but pretty well as general manager. She struggled, as many mainlanders still do, to explain the Chinese approach to 'foreigners'. The word 'foreigner' is applied broadly to all non-mainland Chinese, including those from Hong Kong. All are seen the same rather negative way, as outsiders, lacking any real appreciation of the mainland history, culture or language. Hong Kong might often be mistaken as being 'Chinese' but it is far from it. Language, culture and history are fundamentally different and attitudes clash at many times. Then SARS struck.

The airborne and sometimes fatal disease of SARS (Severe Acute Respiratory Syndrome) hit many countries and businesses very hard. For Tara, it was catastrophic as the Hong Kong business simply cut off the mainland entity and scrapped it in response. It was a time of bitterness for Tara and the team who were willing to work for nothing until the epidemic subsided, but the Hong Kong owners were adamant and closed everything.

In one of the more telling remarks I have heard in China about Hong Kong, Tara's view should be a wakeup call to any business trying to make the Hong Kong linkage to the mainland.

"I decided to leave too. My staff and I couldn't understand the Hong Kong attitude. We didn't like the way they just cynically cut us loose. The Hong Kong attitude was too Western!"

She stayed at home during SARS. It says much for the fortitude, not only of Tara, but of so many Chinese people who suffer setbacks to bounce back or endure what most Westerners would find life-changing and catastrophic. The epidemic which struck southern China officially lasted from November 2002 to July 2003, but the effects were felt for many months later in border controls and heat sensors at all airports across Asia until the official eradication in January 2004. To lose a job for more than a year would be unthinkable in the West, but as many of these Notes attest, it is almost no big deal in China where the family and the strong savings ethic cushion individuals from the worst life can throw at them.

Tara eventually secured a job with DuPont.

"They were a wonderful business. So many of my MBA case studies had been on DuPont. It was just great to be there and experience it for myself. DuPont was my dream company and my dream job. They were selling the business and I was to be there to manage all the HR issues in Beijing through the process. They really cared about their employees and, between 2003 and 2008, I had a really great time. DuPont sold to Koch and I did the transition as everyone moved over. I was responsible for it all. It was after the DuPont business was bought by Koch that I realized that US companies were very different. DuPont had, what seemed to me, a very European approach and style Koch didn't. In five years, they gave no salary increases at all. The sense was, 'if you don't like it here, go somewhere else'. Everything had to be approved by global, we had no discussion or discretion at all. It was a marketing and brand led business and it was very tough. They had a high staff turnover."

Tara and I discuss her experiences of the differences between a European and a US corporate business. Her overall impression, and that of many Chinese people I have met, is not wholly favourable so far as US corporate culture is concerned. There is a generally held view among the Chinese people I have met that many US businesses are too aggressive, too sales-focused and that they don't care about their people. While this is a stereotypical perception, it does seem to be embedded in the minds of many Chinese people. In addition, there is a common perception, probably not always a reality, that US businesses set aside Chinese culture in favour of the 'American way' being the best way forward. Needless to say, this goes down very badly with the Chinese who expect respect and cultural sensitivity from their overseas employers.

There are, of course, many examples where Western businesses have invested in their Chinese staff with amazing results, from customer satisfaction scores to profitability and retention. The numbers say it all and Tara is quite emphatic. Cultural sensitivity wins every time.

Tara left her US employers with no regret and moved to an Italian company where she stayed until the business decided to relocate to Shanghai. She didn't want to leave her elderly parents and, by now, she was married with two young children. The potential wrench would have been too great so she opted to stay in Beijing and leave the business. There were struggles with the Italians during her time there and she recalls a few moments where she had to stand up to Italian male egos, but overall she found herself enjoying the on going, and now long association, with non-Chinese corporate life.

"It was clear to me looking back that I was really always leaning West. It was interesting to find that Westerners might not have expected this tiny Chinese woman to be so tough but we got on fine in the end. The fact I am Chinese has never held me back in a Western company, they didn't care if I was married, or had kids. In fact, DuPont let me take my daughter to work for the few times when our nanny was ill or we didn't have help."

Tara explains to me, throughout our discussions, that labour law in China is quite different from in the West.

"It is a good deal easier to fire someone in the US or in the UK than it is in China. Certainly, if that someone is under-performing and pregnant. The documentary proof required to sever contracts is enormous and no more so than around pregnancy."

The focus on one child, and the importance of family and that child is ingrained in the Chinese psyche. It can take up to two years to sever relations with certain employees and the burden of proof has to be agreed and signed for by the employee if the individual is a pregnant woman. The regulations also differ in substance and in interpretation across China, province by province, city by city and sometimes court by court and even judge by judge. The lesson here is get the right advice in HR and ensure it's localized.

Tara also reflects that "foreign companies find it a lot more difficult to shut up shop and disappear. Local companies can close and/or disappear quite easily, leaving the staff floundering in their wake. Foreign companies, with brand reputations to uphold, find it much more stressful and difficult to manage underperformance and dismissals. If a Chinese company wants to close a branch it can do it inside two weeks. For a foreign company it can take up to two years!"

So I asked her to sum up the lessons from her long and varied past in HR and the, mainly Western, corporate experience in China.

"Be careful what you wish for," she says. "Be careful how you set it up, and be well advised on all fronts so you can manage the risks."

By now, we both feel that, despite the warmth of our coffee, our feet have resisted the cold long enough and it is time to call it a day. As we part, I reflect on the conversation. Tara introduced herself to me as 'Mrs Tara Li', a Western introduction and a Western style of address, for a Westernized and essentially Western experienced professional. It was of little surprise for me to learn that she had married an Englishman, in fact a Yorkshireman (known for their straight-talking and sometimes rude directness). I suspect that Tata has, and will continue to have, a long and happy marriage.

# Against all odds

Wang Li Ran, was born in Beijing in the 1950s. She has had a long, extremely distinguished and well-recognized career in Chinese government departments. Now retired and, rightly, doting on her newly-arrived grandson, she remains one of the most highly respected and acknowledged influencers of the post revolution era inside the accounting and finance profession in China.

We do not meet in my coffeeshop.

The traffic is even more dreadful than normal in Beijing. It is the week of the National People's Congress (NPC) and Chinese People's Political Consultative Conference (CPPCC), the most important annual conferences of the Chinese Government. Security is horrendous and so is the traffic. Chang An avenue, the main thoroughfare past Tiananmen Square and the Great Hall of the People, where the meeting is being held, is, at best, moving at walking pace. It is a bright, sunny, uncharacteristically smog-free, day in the city.

Li Ran is accompanied by her demure and solidly respectful 28 year-old daughter-in-law, who acts as an accomplished translator. Li Ran's English is very good, but she wants to ensure her story is accurately conveyed. Her daughter-in-law's English is perfect, and she is good at French too, I learn. In her typical well-prepared style, always attentive to detail, Li Ran navigates our meeting with self-effacing elegance.

"So, what do you want to ask me?"

I sent my broad areas of questioning to her in advance but this is permission to proceed, and so we do.

"Tell me about your life," I say.

She laughs. She is totally at ease, and over a rather refined coffee in one of the best hotels in Beijing, if not in China, her fascinating story unfolds.

"I was born in Beijing, and right after I graduated from middle school, I was 'dispatched' to a small village nearby Baotou."

Baotou is now one of the biggest industrial centres in the Chinese province of Inner Mongolia, but in those days of her youth, it was only just starting to develop. Li Ran, like so many of her era, was sent to the countryside to use their knowledge to help the local villagers by the Communist regime of the time.

"I was lucky really as I was very young so didn't really find it such a hardship."

The reasons for this emerge later but Li Ran was different. Many youngsters were sent to much harsher and far flung places, often in the crushingly poor areas of South and Western China such as Shanxi and Yunnan province.

"Together with 14 schoolmates, I left Beijing and headed for the small village in Inner Mongolia. That was 1968. In those days, the authorities looked at your background, your family and your situation. I knew that I didn't have a good background at the time, with my grandfather being a landowner and my parents having a small business, so I decided to leave as fast as I could so I would get a better 'despatch' to the countryside. It was the right thing to do. I left a few months early and it helped. Everyone had to leave by December 1968 but I went four months early. Many others had a very bad time and were away for much longer than me. I, however, only spent three years in the village."

For those well versed in the recent history of China the story of the 'despatch', touched on in an earlier chapter, will be well understood, but for those who are not it is worthy of a brief explanation. These were the times of the notorious Red Guard, there was significant disruption across China, but no more so in the cities, and at its most bloody and sometimes brutal, in Beijing itself. Different factions of the Red Guard and the Youth League were vying, sometimes even fighting, with one another to flush out the bourgeoisie and 'undesirable' elements in society, which included 'intellectuals'. There are countless stories of landowners, big and small, being required to hand over land and give up wealth, often hard-gained, in the name of the Revolution. Li Ran's parents and family fell into that category of wealth, which was not deemed appropriate in the new order. Many parents resisted the Great Despatch, hiding their children's Hukou (residency) documents to forestall their being sent away. Few avoided it and many suffered being sent to much harsher places than Li Ran as a result of the understandable deception of their fearful parents. This is a generation, which was lost to the education system, as the schools closed and didn't reopen until 1971. The effect on the China of today is still visible in many ways.

"My parents had hidden the Hukou of my brother when the despatch had been called. In my class of 45 students, only one or two managed to avoid the despatch and stay in Beijing due to their family situation, or special circumstances. Everyone else had to leave. Like I said, I left early to help the situation for my family."

What was it like?

"I was lucky, as the people in Inner Mongolia at that time had a perception of women that meant they did not really expect us to work. So we learned to do the work we did part time and knit some sweaters in our spare time which we then gave to the locals as gifts to show our respect and gratitude. We received no money. In return they often gave us food. It was a good natured exchange. Life as a part-time worker in the village was a good deal easier than that which many of my classmates, and many others of my age group, had to endure across China.

"I then went to normal school in Baotou. I was 20 years old. I had four months at school until the end of the Cultural Revolution, training to be a teacher. Then I went to a middle school in Baotou. It was one of the best middle schools in the region. I spent three-and-a-half years there as a teacher. I then went to Tianjin University of Economics and Finance. The reason I wanted to go to college was that, compared with the elder teachers of that middle school, my education level was relatively low. I couldn't have been selected if it hadn't been for the lack of teachers in the post-revolution era. So it's always been my goal to attend college."

I am confused. How did she manage to get to Tianjin University, one of the best in China, having been a teacher trained in the middle of nowhere in Inner Mongolia?

"I'll tell you. I was recommended by the Baotou school to go to the university. They had the chance to recommend people. There were 28 teachers in all of the Baotou Middle Schools who were thought good enough to be recommended to be sent to university. Only five were chosen and I was one of them. The Education Bureau in Baotou held a meeting to discuss the performance of their best teachers and to see who should be selected. I was one of them. I was so delighted. I was highly recommended by the middle school and my fellow students who made representations at the time to encourage the Education Bureau to accept me. There were meetings of the students to support my going forward."

I am genuinely amazed. I am more than well aware from studying both ancient and recent Chinese history that local meetings were convened for most things in China. I had never heard of a meeting convened specifically to support the application of one, no doubt gifted, student to be sent to university. But that was the case with Li Ran. The reason for the strong support needs to be grounded in the history of the time, which requires the reader to spend a good deal of extra time in study, but the bottom line is that local groups had the power and ability to influence local affairs in ways that some Westerners might find frighteningly democratic.

"When I started working, I thought I was not good enough," she continues. "So I really worked hard. I worked every day until midnight, sometimes later. I was an art teacher and I painted all the slogans and loyal [Communist Party propaganda] pictures in our school. Before me, there had been a painting teacher but he had not had the energy to paint as strongly as me. People saw the difference immediately. I was lucky to have skill and put the effort in to be as good as I could be. I really cherished the opportunity to be a teacher and I had had a bit of a hard life in the village in the countryside so I really wanted to excel."

She did and her diligence and dedication to the cause, the painting and the school, were clearly recognized and appreciated by all around her.

"The headmaster went personally to the Education Bureau to recommend me for the university opportunity. They chose me."

I have to say, against this extraordinary wall of genuine affection and admiration, based on her hard work and skill, it would have been very unlikely that the Bureau would have turned her down. Possible, yes, but unlikely.

"I graduated from Tianjin University with a major in finance. The teaching staff then recommended that I be sent to the Ministry of Finance."

As you can read elsewhere in this book, students at that time were allocated jobs by the University as an arm of government. Li Ran was no different, so in 1978 her cherished Hukou (permit of residence) was moved back to Beijing (it followed her from the village to Baotou, from Baotou to Tianjin, then to Beijing).

She was back home.

"My Hukou had been away from Beijing for 10 years."

There is a pause from all of us around the low coffee table. I am aware of being totally absorbed in the story. Outside, the sun shines brightly and the plush limos and taxis disgorge their wealthy visitors in a seemingly endless procession of high heels and leather briefcases. We sit in post-Revolution China and reflect on life, history and change.

"I'm interested in your name," I say, thinking it is time to move on. "Wang Li Ran is an unusual name. I know names reflect the hopes and dreams of parents for their children, what was the origin of your name?" This is a super sensitive question in China, steeped in meaning.

"My father gave it to me," she replies. "As a direct translation it means 'beautiful nature' but it has deeper meaning as well, as a status of beauty and beautiful gestures, the appearance of beauty. My father had great hopes for me. He was a teacher before the liberation of the People's Republic of China. There is a story that when I became a teacher in Baotou Middle School, my sister wrote to my father to tell him of my achievements. He was so proud of me, he went around the streets telling people that his daughter had become a teacher."

Her father's pride is understandable in the context of China at that time, just after the Revolution. To have a daughter achieve so much, step in the shoes of her teacher father and succeed not only so far from home, but so well, must have seemed to be the pinnacle of an impossible dream. Against the odds of the time, Li Ran had been hugely successful. He was rightly proud.

"Ten of my classmates from university were allocated to the Ministry of Finance with me. We were allocated all over the department, but because I had been a teacher and a painter of slogans I was allocated to the central administration department. Because of my skills and the good name I had managed to create, the leaders of the ministry allocated me to be an editor. Every conference and big meeting had to have slogans and paintings produced. I was allocated the task of producing these for all the big meetings and conferences. I painted a lot of slogans."

I am judicious in my questions but it does emerge that Li Ran was not only good at painting slogans but probably the best at doing so.

"I painted the slogan for the very first founding meeting of the CICPA (Chinese Institute of Certified Public Accountants). Actually, I should say that I re-painted the slogan as the person who had done it did not do a good job and the leaders felt my painting was better, so I re-did it. I still have the photograph of all the leaders in front of my slogan. I became famous in the ministry then for this, and for my ability to take photographs too. As an editor, I also helped with the founding of the first ever finance magazine in China. That was in October 1978."

The magazine was a runaway success. Under Li Ran's editorship, the Finance and Accounting Magazine became a must-read publication for all those involved in the finance profession in China. She was very well known as editor for more than 10 years.

"We produced the first trial edition in 1979 and it had a print run of 400,000 copies. We managed to get it to a maximum circulation of 700,000 copies when I left. It doesn't have that now, however. I then transferred to the CICPA in 1993, in charge of the training and examination department. In May 1995, I was promoted to the role of deputy secretary general by the ministry. We launched the CICPA magazine in 1999 with me as chief editor, and I kept that job until I retired in February 2011."

She pauses and beams at me. This is an amazing achievement and she knows it. During her tenure as editors of the two magazines, the finance and accounting profession in China was born and grew up. She witnessed some of the most significant changes in China and was at the heart of one of the most important and influential departments and groups navigating the unchartered waters of an emerging profession in an emerging economic superpower. No wonder she is a tiny bit proud.

"When I retired from CICPA, as all officials have to do at 60, I felt that I still had a lot of energy and wanted to contribute and saw a need to help bridge the Chinese accounting profession to the western world. Then… about the same time ICAEW (Institute of Chartered Accountants of England and Wales) was looking to expand their presence in China. They were familiar friends as when I was working at CICPA I'd also helped ICAEW come to China. So after I joined the ICAEW, I helped arranged multiple exchanging programmes between the two organizations, which have been widely welcomed by the Chinese accounting professionals."

"What differences did you experience between the Chinese way and the British way?" I tiptoe through the question.

"Oh really not so different. Chinese people and British people have many similarities. We both have a long and distinguished history. We have a culture of courtesy and generosity. We share a lot in common. Unlike the US."

Again, I am intrigued by the perceived differences the Chinese see between the US and UK, let alone other counties.

"Our English teacher at CICPA was English (English courses, among many others, were and still are offered to employees at the Ministry of Finance and many other government departments). Our teacher talked a lot about the differences between the US and the UK, not just language, but culture too.

"I have been very lucky to travel a good deal because of my job. I often read about the Chinese abroad behaving very badly. But I think the media exaggerates these stories to stir up bad perceptions of the Chinese. I went to the US in 1994 and Malaysia in 1998. Many of the young people we met thought we were Korean or Japanese. They couldn't tell the difference! Now people can tell the difference. The Chinese are the ones with the money. Everyone knows that the Chinese have wealth and cash to spend and the old historical perceptions are changing."

Li Ran tells me a story to illustrate her point.

"In 2002, my son, my only son under the one-child policy, went to France to college. One day he called me. He was really angry. Some fellow students had been asking him if he slept on a mud bench with a fire underneath it at home to keep him warm. He said to me 'mother send me photographs of our apartment so I can show these people what it is really like!' so I did and they were amazed that we had, and have, modern apartments with beds and chairs and sofas, washing machines and so on. Just like them. We laugh now but it was serious. People really didn't know anything about China except the old negative perceptions from years and years ago. His class-mates needed to be educated.

"There are two extreme perceptions in the West of China: first that we are poor and they look down on us; second that we are the biggest threat in the world. Since China has grown so fast in the past 10-15 years, the story is one of worry and fear."

My understanding of Li Ran's comments is that the seemingly widely held Western perspective on China is the worry surrounding both its military and economic might.

Another, rather more serious story.

"Another classmate of my son was a very diligent student. She got an internship working for a French car manufacturer. She was trying to finish work at the end of a day and decided that she would finish it at home that evening. She took the computer home with her to do the work in her apartment. She was arrested by the French police and put in prison. She was suspected of being a Chinese spy. It was all over the French and Chinese media. It happened that her parents lived in Shiyan, which was a car manufacturing centre in China. They believed that she was stealing intellectual property from the French company. It was total rubbish. My son knew her as a diligent and good student. That was it. She spent six months in a French prison. It was a devastating life experience for her."

One has to hope that those days of misunderstanding and misperception are dying out, though I fear not entirely. It's good to get a view from the average, and not so average, person on the ground. In China, stereotypes of other countries are as deep-seated as they are in other countries about China. However, they certainly want the perceptions to change and all the Chinese people I know are far more educated about the rest of the world than the rest of the world is about China.

"Personally, I have always tried to help people, even if they don't help me back," says Li Ran. "I've always found I get more out of life that way. Through being an editor and being in charge of the training department at the CICPA

I was so very lucky to meet many different people. I know a lot of people. This has given me very rewarding connections and relationships all over the world as well as in China. I have tried to use those relationships to help the people I know. At the ICAEW I was happy to use my contacts to help them develop their position here in China. It is a great institution and very prestigious, as I said. I was proud to work with them and help them develop and grow here."

Even now, fully retired from all her paid working life, Li Ran is called upon to provide unpaid advice and is regularly consulted by many, including myself, on matters relating to the accounting profession in China. She does this because she wants to help and does it willingly. Li Ran is unique amongst many retired Chinese, especially retired from official positions, as it is extremely rare for them to return to any form of work, let alone for an international organization. Li Ran is special. The last of Li Ran's stories she told in response to my asking her what she was most proud of in her life?

"My son has turned out to be a good boy. People ask me how I raised such a good son. I just say that he is a reflection of me and my values. Not to be selfish and to think of others. I let my only son, my boy, grow up for himself, without too many boundaries. My son went to France in 2002 as you know. He didn't come back to visit until 2004. He didn't come back in 2004 for the Chinese New Year, which is a very important time for Chinese families. I called him and asked him why not. He said he couldn't come home at that time but would come home later in the year. Then he told me the reason. At that time, he was working in a restaurant to earn some money for his study and his life in France. In 2004, the Chinese New Year fell over the 14 February. When he told his boss that he wanted to go home for the Chinese New Year his boss asked him to stay as there would be a very big increase in trade at Valentine's Day and he needed him to help. My son said he would stay and help, and when my son told me, I supported his decision. He was thinking just the same as me. I was very proud of him.

"I am very proud of him now too. Through the one-child policy, many children are turning out to be selfish. People blame the politics. I don't. I believe it is more about the parenting skills."

She turns to her daughter-in-law and smiles warmly.

Additional note:

The reader should be aware that I have used Wang Li Ran's personal name throughout these Notes and I hope she is happy that I have. I should really refer to her with more respect and she would normally be addressed as Wang laoshi (teacher) or Wang shuji (party secretary) to reflect a role she held for many years in the CICPA. To me, she has simply been Madam Wang, or in moments of real friendship, 'Linda'. I know she prefers her Chinese name, which is why it is used here throughout as my own personal mark of respect to this extraordinary woman.

# AUTUMN

It's hot in the coffeeshop now.

Being someone who never likes operating at anything over 0 degrees since my time in the Arctic, it is snug beyond reason.

The date is 16 November and the heating in Beijing was turned on, by local government decree, yesterday. I forgot the date and expected to need the woollen black polo neck that I thought looked rather cool, but is decidedly not. Back to layers tomorrow.

I make a mental note. I guess I'll complain too in March next year when it goes off again - always too early!

# A letter to the reader

Dear reader,

If you are browsing to the back, or have finished and turned the last page, I am grateful for your time.

I am not in Beijing.

I am not in my favourite Beijing coffeeshop.

I am in another coffeeshop more than 8,350km from Beijing.

The internet is working, the noise of cups and coffee is much the same but I am in my home town of Harrogate in Yorkshire in the North of England. In China, the Lantern Festival has just finished and people are back at work with a vengeance after the long Chinese New Year Festival break. Lantern Festival marks the last day of the lunar New Year celebrations. It is 15 days after Chinese New Year and this year (2015) it is as late as it can ever be, New Year falling on 19 February and Lantern festival on 5 March.

A year has passed since I last sat here and started to write Notes. I am sitting and thinking; reflecting on the many people I have met and stories I have heard, noted and recorded in Beijing, many of them now included here, though some still languish in the dog-eared pages of my note books, a few respecting their post-interview request of anonymity.

The stories keep coming and I am still receiving invitations to interview, and probably will. The story of modern China and modern Beijing continues to unfold every day in the honest and uncensored words of the ordinary Chinese people to whom I talk. I sat and listened, they sat and talked. The coffee and location was a metaphor for our differences but also for our similarities. The Western foreigner and the indigenous Chinese. Very different, yet so similar in so many ways. We are human beings, we share the same emotions and the same needs, though we do not share the same history, language or culture. The seeming gulf between us, I feel, is more in our perception than in reality. A willingness to talk and share, to seek out common ground, was a solid bridge which overcame almost all of the misunderstanding and stereotypical prejudices we both initially brought to our shared coffees.

I have been incredibly fortunate to have been able to meet the people I have met and even more privileged that they have shared their stories and thoughts.

I have tried very hard to act as a mirror, true and fair, to the shared confidences, dreams and perspectives of my interviewees. I have, no doubt, made some errors. I trust they will forgive me for those. These Notes are my own, including the personal reflections on life in China and Chinese life. They are not an official or corporate review or assessment, certainly not a full audit of China, but they are my genuine perspectives and views on what I have heard and experienced.

I hope you find them of value and of interest.

Let me know.

Kind regards,

Jonathan

# An introduction to
## Jonathan Geldart

Jonathan Geldart was born in Pembrokeshire in Wales in 1958 and brought up in Yorkshire in the north of England. The son of a Professor in chemical engineering, he gained his MA at St Andrews University in geography and archaeology, specializing in underwater archaeology. After a short time training to be a brewer, he went on to pursue a career in marketing. Outside work, he competed in motor rally sport for almost 20 years, eventually at an international level, but his real passion is the outdoors and exploration. In 2006, he was part of a team that trekked unsupported for 26 days in sub-zero temperatures to the Geo Magnetic North Pole from Canada. He has climbed in the Himalayas and undertaken expeditions in Norway and the Canadian Arctic. In his 'spare' time he still runs leadership training and team development courses for business people that requires them to climb mountains and sleep outside, often in sub-zero temperatures. He is a Fellow of The Royal Geographical Society and a council member of The British Exploring Society.

Jonathan started working in packaged goods for major blue chip consumer brands and subsequently focused on professional services where he spent significant time within two of the largest firms in the world in various strategic, marketing and business development roles. At PwC, he ended a 16-year distinguished career, as UK marketing director for their mid-market practice, joining Grant Thornton International Ltd. in 2006 to become international marketing director.

Having spent a number of years with extended visits to China, in 2013, Grant Thornton International Ltd. appointed him as executive director, markets development, with a specific remit in emerging markets, and China in particular. He has now worked in China, off and on, for more than five years and on a more extended basis since 2013.

Jonathan is captivated by China as an economy, by its long history and fascinating culture but, in particular, by the people. Everyone has a compelling story and this book tells some of them.

Together, they serve to paint a picture of China through the eyes of real Chinese people who represent all ages, social groups and backgrounds.

Through a series of interviews conducted mostly in his favourite Beijing coffeeshop, Jonathan simply asked a few questions and let the people speak. What he learned was insightful and compelling and is recorded here for the reader to draw their own conclusions and some additional insights from the words of those interviewed, coupled with a personal commentary from Jonathan.

He decided to write this book as a follow-up to *The Thoughts of Chairmen Now*, a book he co-authored with David Roth from WPP plc, the world's largest communications group with multiple businesses across China.

*The Thoughts of Chairmen Now* was a different sort of business book. It used the stories and words of CEOs and chairmen in China to add colour and human interest to the miracle that is China's emergence as the world's second, soon to be largest, global economy.

This new book of Notes has business content but it is not a pure business book. Nor is it a Beijing guide book, although it provides an insight into life in this extraordinary city. It is a book for anyone interested in China who wants to see beyond the obvious, and often extraordinary, facts and figures. It is written in 'bite-sized' segments so the reader can dip in and out as they wish. It is also short enough to finish in a single sitting, or during a plane journey.

# Acknowledgements

Most books have this page, dedicated to those who provided inspiration, guided and cajoled, translated and edited, encouraged, mentored and soothed ragged nerves and the frayed edges of the beleaguered author. I have to say I was surprised by the ease with which this book has written itself. That is not to say it was easy, but the people who made the difference are those in the book who gave me their trust and their stories. Without their candour and openness, honesty and warmth it would still be a thin pile of discarded napkins next to stale coffee mugs in a Beijing coffeeshop. So, thanks are primarily and overwhelmingly given to them. Joyce Chao must have a special mention as without her support I would have fallen at the first hurdle.

I would also like to buy Paul Gordon, long-time business and personal coach as well as friend, a coffee. Ideally in Beijing, which he has never visited, but where he feels he must have been following the hours of emails, texts, phone calls and breakfasts we had during the months I wrote at weekends and evenings as well as the odd long haul flight between Beijing and London.

Finally I must thank Grant Thornton International Ltd. for allowing me the opportunity to work in China and for the funding to make this idea a reality. You can read elsewhere what the organisation does but suffice to say here that its brand promise is to unlock the potential for growth in dynamic organisations. It also aims to unlock the potential of individuals within it and the clients served by its member firms around the globe. For anyone wanting to visit, do business or simply understand more about China I hope this book goes some way to unlocking insights into an amazing country and its people.